A NEW GRAMMAR

OF THE

HINDOOSTANEE LANGUAGE

A NEW GRAMMAR

OF THE

HINDOOSTANEE LANGUAGE

WILLIAM PRICE

GYAN

Published by

Gyan Publishing House
5, Ansari Road
Daryaganj, New Delhi-110002
Phone: 011-47034999, 9811692060
E-mail: books@gyanbooks.com

Distribution Network
gyanbooks.com
India, USA, Canada, UK, Australia

ISBN: 978-93-6920-319-2 (HB)

First Published, 1823

2nd Impression 2025

Printed at: Gyan Press, Delhi.

A NEW GRAMMAR OF THE HINDOOSTANEE LANGUAGE
Author: WILLIAM PRICE

A NEW GRAMMAR

OF THE

HINDOOSTANEE LANGUAGE.

TO WHICH ARE ADDED,

SELECTIONS FROM THE BEST AUTHORS,

FAMILIAR PHRASES, AND DIALOGUES,

IN THE PROPER CHARACTER.

BY WILLIAM PRICE. M. R. S. L.

ASSISTANT SECRETARY TO THE RIGHT HONORABLE SIR GORE OUSELEY, BART.
AMBASSADOR EXTRAORDINARY AND MINISTER PLENIPOTENTIARY
FROM HIS BRITANNIC MAJESTY TO THE COURT OF PERSIA.

LONDON.

PUBLISHED BY PARBURY, ALLEN, AND CO, BOOKSELLERS TO THE HONORABLE
EAST INDIA COMPANY, LEADENHALL STREET.

1828.

PREFACE.

The hindoostanee is a modern dialect, partly derived from the sanscrit, and partly from the arabic and persian. The hindoos preserve a greater mixture of sanscrit, while the mussulman part of the people tincture their expressions with an unlimited number of arabic and persian words and phrases. It therefore requires a partial knowledge of sanscrit, arabic, and persian, to be perfectly acquainted with hindoostanee: for this reason, I have composed an elementary grammar of the sanscrit language, as an accompaniment to this; by which the hindoostanee may be traced to the fountain-head. Particular care has been taken to render the rules clear and concise, which, with a moderate application, may be soon learned. As to the arabic and persian, all that is requisite for the acquirement of the former, will be found in my GRAMMAR OF THE THREE PRINCIPAL ORIENTAL LANGUAGES, published in 1823. A very useful set of dialogues in persian and english will be found in that book, and a few rules towards persian grammar; but I may probably be induced to publish at a future period, a more complete grammar of the persian language, upon an improved plan.

CONTENTS,

CORRECTIONS.

Page 25 dele numerals; being repeated under the figures in page 94.

8 *line* 20 *for* بهوت *write* بهت P 90 *l* 15 *for comming wr coming*

LETTERS OR CHARACTERS.

The hindoostanee, like the persian, is written variously, according to the fancies of transcribers. Sometimes in the plain niskhi, and sometimes in letters of other shapes. Even in printed works the learner is often impeded by a variety of certain characters; I shall therefore lay down a few of the most common not introduced into the alphabet as, ے or ـــے for ی or ي ; يل for ي when ي takes the sound of ا ; بجـ for بجـ and so with all others of the same class. مر for ر ; مز for ز ; مژ for ژ ; ﻻ for لا ; سه for سه ; گ for گ with a few others to be learned by practice.

VOWEL POINTS AND OTHER SIGNS.

The short vowels are generally omitted in composition, being understood, as they are in arabic and persian; but being used on some occasions, they must be learned as well as the long vowels.

There are three short vowels; called *fatha*, *dhamma*, *casra*; the first is expressed by this mark ´ over a consonant as دَ *dă* or *dĕ*, the second by a sort of coma over as دُ *dŭ*; the third, by a mark under, as دِ *dĭ*; the long vowels corresponding with these, are ي و ا. The other signs are these:—ْ *jezma*, placed over a consonant, shows no vowel follows it. ~ *medda* over ا so آ, gives it a broad sound. ٔ *hamza* supplies the place of ا or ي ّ *teshdeed* over a letter, shows it is double. ٱ *wesla* over *alif* so ٱ marks a union with the preceding vowel, alif itself being silent. The three following are called *tenween*, ٌ ٍ ً, pronounced *on*, *in*, *an*; they are signs of the cases Nom. Gen. Acc. in arabic words.

Arabic characters have in this language been generally adopted, with seven additional letters borrowed from the sanscrit and persian: they are thirty five in number, and are written from right to left in the following order.

THE HINDOOSTANEE ALPHABET.

	FINALS. Connected	FINALS. Unconnected.	MEDIALS. Connected.	INITIALS. Unconnected.	
Alif	ـا	ا	ـا	ا	A
Ba	ـب	ب	ـبـ	بـ	B
Pa	ـپ	پ	ـپـ	پـ	P
Ta	ـت	ت	ـتـ	تـ	T
Ta	ـٹ	ٹ	ـٹـ	ٹـ	T
Sa	ـث	ث	ـثـ	ثـ	S
Jeem	ـج	ج	ـجـ	جـ	J
Cheem	ـچ	چ	ـچـ	چـ	Ch
Hha	ـح	ح	ـحـ	حـ	Hh
Kha	ـخ	خ	ـخـ	خـ	Kh
Dal	ـد	د	ـد	د	D
Da	ـڈ	ڈ	ـڈ	ڈ	D
Ra	ـڑ	ڑ	ـڑ	ڑ	R
Zal	ـذ	ذ	ـذ	ذ	Z
Ra	ـر	ر	ـر	ر	R

These nine letters must not be joined with letters that follow them.

ا د ڈ ڑ ذ ر ز ژ و

	FINALS. Connected.	Unconnected.	MEDIALS. Connected.	INITIALS. Unconnected.	
Za	ـز	ز	ـز	ز	Z
Zha	ـژ	ژ	ـژ	ژ	Zh
Seen	ـس	س	ـسـ	سـ	S
Sheen	ـش	ش	ـشـ	شـ	Sh
Saad	ـص	ص	ـصـ	صـ	Ss
Zaad	ـض	ض	ـضـ	ضـ	Zz
Ta	ـط	ط	ـطـ	طـ	T
Zaa	ـظ	ظ	ـظـ	ظـ	Z
Ain	ـع	ع	ـعـ	عـ	Aa
Ghain	ـغ	غ	ـغـ	غـ	Gh
Fa	ـف	ف	ـفـ	فـ	F
Kaf	ـق	ق	ـقـ	قـ	K
Kiaf	ـک	ک	ـکـ	کـ	K
Gaf	ـگ	گ	ـگـ	گـ	G
Lam	ـل	ل	ـلـ	لـ	L
Meem	ـم	م	ـمـ	مـ	M
Noon	ـن	ن	ـنـ	نـ	N
Vau	ـو	و	ـو	و	V
Ha	ـه	ه	ـهـ	هـ	H
Ya	ـي	ي	ـيـ	يـ	Y
Lam-alif	ـلا	لا	ـلا	لا	

ON PRONUNCIATION.

The letter ا, at the beginning of words, sounds like *a* in *an*; but in the middle and end of words, it has a broad sound, like that of *aw* in *fawn*: when written at the beginning of a word thus, آ it takes the broad sound. ب پ ت the same as *b*, *p*, *t*, in english. ٹ the sanscrit letter ट a sort of *t*, expressed by turning the tip of the tongue to the back of the palate. ث this letter has in arabic the sound of *th* in *thistle*, but in this language it is pronounced like the common *s*. ج as *j* in *joy*. چ as *ch* in *chin*. ح as *h* or *hh*, it being strongly aspirated. خ a strong gutural sound answering to the greek χ or the german *ch*. د the common *d*. ڈ and ڑ the sanscrit letter ड which sometimes takes the sound of *d*, and sometimes that of *r*, with the tongue reverted on the palate as described above. ذ another *z*; ر, ز the common *r* and *z*; ژ this letter expresses the soft sound given to *j* by the french, or *s* in *pleasure*. س the common *s*; ش *sh* in *ship*; ص a strong *s*; ض another *z*; ط another *t*; ظ *z*; ع a deep toned *a* corresponding with the hebrew ע; غ *gh* pronounced gutturally, like *r* by the Northumbrians; ف common *f*; ق a harsh-sounded *k*, by placing the root of the tongue to the back of the palate and drawing it suddenly away. ک as *k* in *king*; گ *g* in *go*; ل *l* in *letter*; م *m* in *meet*; ن *n* in *net*; و *v* in *virtue*, or *oo* in *pool*; ه *h* in *hurt*; ی *y* in *yellow*; لا the letters *l* and *a* joined in one and sounded *la*. The aspirated consonants of the sanscrit are in hindoostanee, expressed as in roman characters, which is, by putting ھ *h* after the simple consonant, as ख *k,h* کھ घ *g,h* گھ छ *ch,h* چھ झ *j,h* جھ ठ *t,h* ٹھ ढ *d,h* ڈھ or ڑھ थ *t,h* تھ ध *d,h* دھ फ *p,h* پھ भ *b,h* بھ

GRAMMAR

OF THE

Hindoostanee Language.

ARTICLE.

Like the Persian, this language has no regular Article; but the words ايك one, يهي this, and وه that, are often used to denote it.

NOUNS.

All Nouns are either masculine or feminine by signification or termination: those ending in ا or ه are generally masculine, and such as end in ي are, for the most part, feminine.

Names of countries, hills, woods, seas, lakes, days, months, letters, &c. are masculine; some things are considered both masculine and feminine, as موسم a season, جان life, گهاو a wound; and doubtful words, though feminine, may be treated as masculine.

Feminines are formed from masculine nouns by changing ا or ه into ي as چچا an uncle, چچي an aunt, شهزاده a prince, شهزادي a princess; and sometimes by ني as ملا a schoolmaster, ملاني a schoolmistress, هندو a Hindoo, هندوني a female Hindoo.

Masculine Nouns ending in ي generally form their feminines by changing ي into ن as دهوبي a washerman, دهوبن a washerwoman.

Those ending with a consonant form their feminines variously, as سنار a goldsmith, سنارن a goldsmith's wife, شير a tiger, شيرني a tigress, سور a boar, سوري a sow.

In common with other eastern languages, this acknowledges but three cases; but, conformably to our own method of declension, modern grammarians have made them six.

DECLENSIONS.

The declensions are very simple, and may be reduced to few rules; the following are the principal forms:—

	SINGULAR.		PLURAL.	
N.	كاندها	a shoulder.	كاندهے	shoulders.
G.	كاندهے كا كے كي	of a shoulder.	كاندهوں كا كے كي	of shoulders.
D.	كاندهے كو	to a shoulder.	كاندهوں كو	to shoulders.
Ac.	كاندهے كو	the shoulder.	كاندهوں كو	the shoulders.
V.	اي كاندهے	O shoulder.	اي كاندهو	O shoulders.
Ab.	كاندهے سے	from a shoulder.	كاندهوں سے	from shoulders.

The termination ا or ه being changed to ے forms the plural of most nouns, with the exception of the following: راجا a king, ملا a teacher, امرا a nobleman, خدا God, بابا a father, استا a barber, پتا a father, پيا a husband, كبتا a poet, ميرزا a man of letters, گدا a beggar, دانا a wise man, سودا a melancholy man, and a few others, which are declined thus—

	SINGULAR.		PLURAL.	
N.	راجا	a king.	راجا	kings.
G.	راجا كا كے كي	of a king.	راجاوں كا كے كي	of kings.
D.	راجا كو	to a king.	راجاوں كو	to kings.
Ac.	راجا كو	the king.	راجاوں كو	the kings.
V.	اي راجا	O king.	اي راجاو	O kings.
Ab.	راجا سے	from a king.	راجاوں سے	from kings.

	SINGULAR.		PLURAL.	
N.	رنڈي	a woman.	رنڈياں	women.
G.	رنڈي کا کے کي	of a woman.	رنڈيوں کا کے کي	of women.
D.	رنڈي کو	to a woman.	رنڈيوں کو	to women.
Ac.	رنڈي کو	the woman.	رنڈيوں کو	the women.
V.	اي رنڈي	O woman.	اي رنڈيو	O women.
Ab.	رنڈي سے	from a woman.	رنڈيوں سے	from women.

	SINGULAR.		PLURAL.	
N.	بندہ	a servant.	بندے	servants.
G.	بندے کا کے کي	of a servant.	بندوں کا کے کي	of servants.
D.	بندے کو	to a servant.	بندوں کو	to servants.
Ac.	بندے کو	the servant.	بندوں کو	the servants.
V.	اي بندے	O servant.	اي بندو	O servants.
Ab.	بندے سے	from a servant.	بندوں سے	from servants.

	SINGULAR.		PLURAL.	
N.	رات	a night.	راتيں	nights.
G.	رات کا کے کي	of a night.	راتوں کا کے کي	of nights.
D.	رات کو	to a night.	راتوں کو	to nights.
Ac.	رات کو	the night.	راتوں کو	the nights.
V.	اي رات	O night.	اي راتو	O nights.
Ab.	رات سے	from a night.	راتوں سے	from nights.

ADJECTIVES.

Adjectives accord with their substantives in gender and number, and generally precede them, as

	SINGULAR.		PLURAL.	
N.	کالا لنڈا	a black boy.	کالے لنڈے	black boys.
G.	کالے لنڈے کا کے کي		کالے لنڈوں کا کے کي	
D.	کالے لنڈے کو		کالے لنڈوں کو	
Ac.	کالے لنڈے کو		کالے لنڈوں کو	
V.	اي کالے لنڈے		اي کالے لنڈو	
Ab.	کالے لنڈے سے		کالے لنڈوں سے	

	SINGULAR.		PLURAL.	
N.	کالي لنڈي	a black girl.	کالي لنڈياں	black girls.
G.	کالي لنڈي کا کي کي		کالي لنڈيوں کا کے کي	
D.	کالي لنڈي کو		کالي لنڈيوں کو	
Ac.	کالي لنڈي کو		کالي لنڈيوں کو	
V.	اي کالي لنڈي		اي کالي لنڈو	
Ab.	کالي لنڈي سے		کالي لنڈيوں سے	

پانچواں دن the fifth day.

The comparative and superlative degrees are expressed by سے than, مین among, مین سے from among, کا of بہوت much, بڑا great, زیادہ or اؤر more, نپٹ نہایت or اتي extremely, حد excessively, بسا most, very, &c. or by repeating the positive as اچھا اچھا better, اچھا سے اچھا best.

Sometimes the Persian comparatives are used, as بہ good, بہتر better, بہترین best.

The Persian affix سا which means resemblance, generally changes its final to ي when governing nouns feminine, and so with other adjuncts ending in ا

PRONOUNS.

First Person.

	SINGULAR.		PLURAL.	
N.	میں	I.	هم	we.
G.	میرا میری میري	my, of me.	همارا هماری هماري	our, of us.
D.	مجهکو or مجهے	to me.	همکو or همیں	to us.
Ac.	مجهکو or مجهي	me.	همکو or همیں	us.
Ab.	مجهسے	from me.	هم سے	from us.

Second Person.

	SINGULAR.		PLURAL.	
N.	تو or تیں	thou.	تم	you.
G.	تیرا تیری تیري	thy, of thee.	تمهارا تمهاری تمهاري	your, of you.
D.	تجهکو or تجهے	to thee.	تم کو or تمهیں	to you.
Ac.	تجهکو or تجهے	thee.	تمکو or تمهیں	you.
V.	اي تو	O thou,	اي تم	O you.
Ab.	تجهسے	from thee.	تم سے	from you.

Third Person.

	SINGULAR.		PLURAL.	
N.	وه	he, she, it.	وي	they.
G.	اس کا کے کي	of him, &c.	اُن کا کے کي	of them.
D.	اس کو or اسے	to him.	اُن کو or انهیں	to them.
Ac.	اسکو or اسے	him, &c.	انکو or انهیں	them.
Ab.	اس سے	from him.	اُن سے	from them.

	SINGULAR.		PLURAL.	
N.	يه	this.	يے	these.
G.	اِس کا کے کي	of this.	اِن کا کے کي	of these.
D.	اِس کو or اسے	to this.	اِن کو or اِنهيں	to these.
Ac.	اسکو or اسے	this.	انکو or انهيں	these.
Ab.	اس سے	from this.	اِن سے	from these.

REFLECTIVE PRONOUN.

SINGULAR AND PLURAL.

N.	آپ	self, myself, thyself. &c.
G.	آپ کا کے کي or اپنا اپنے اپني	of myself, &c.
D.	آپ کو or اپنے کو	to myself.
Ac.	آپکو or اپنيکو	myself.
Ab.	آپ سے or اپنيسے	from myself.

آپس also means self, but it is generally used in a plural sense, as آپس مين سے from among themselves, ourselves, &c.

THE INTERROGATIVE.

	SINGULAR.		PLURAL.	
N.	کون	who? which? what?	کون	who? which?
G.	کِس کا کے کي	of whom?	کِن کا کے کي	of whom?
D.	کِس کو or کسے	to whom?	کِن کو or کنهين	to whom?
Ac.	کسکو or کسے	whom?	کِنکو or کنهيں	whom?
Ab.	کس سے	from whom?	کِن سے	from whom?

کون for the most part relates to persons, and کيا to things.

SINGULAR AND PLURAL.

N.	كيا	what?
G.	كاهے كا كے كي	of what?
D.	كاهے كو	to what?
Ac.	كاهيكو	what?
Ab.	كاهيسے	from what?

THE RELATIVE.

	SINGULAR.		PLURAL.	
N.	جو or جون	who, which.	جو or جون	who, which.
G.	جِس كا كے كي	of whom.	جِنكا كے كي	of whom.
D.	جِس كو or جسے	to whom.	جِنكو or جِنهين	to whom.
Ac.	جسكو or جسے	whom.	جنكو or جنهين	whom.
Ab.	جس سے	from whom.	جِن سے	from whom.

	SINGULAR.		PLURAL.	
N.	تون or سو	this, that, he, she.	تون or سو	these, those.
G.	تِس كا كے كي	of this.	تِن كا كے كي	of these.
D.	تس كو or تسي	to this.	تِنكو or تنهين	to these.
Ac.	تسكو or تسي	this.	تنكو or تنهين	these.
Ab.	تِس سے	from this, &c.	تِن سے	from these.

	SINGULAR.		PLURAL.	
N.	كوئي	some, any, certain.	كچهه	some.
G.	كسي كا كے كي	of some.	كسو كا كے كي	of some.
D.	كِسي كو	to some.	كِسو كو	to some.
Ac.	كسيكو	some.	كسوكو	some.
Ab.	كِسي سے	from some.	كسوسے	from some.

In like manner may be declined جوي whoever, جوكوي any one, كچھ نهين nothing, اۆركون what else? كتنا how many? جتنا as many, اتنا so much, تتنا this much, &c.

VERB.

The imperative of the second person singular is the root, and by the addition of نا, تا, &c. the infinitive, the participles, and the tenses are formed. The root is often used as a verbal noun.

هونا to be.

Indicative Present.

SINGULAR.		PLURAL.	
مين هوتا هون	I am.	هم هوتے هين	we are.
تو هوتا هي	thou art.	تم هوتے هو	you are.
وه هوتا هي	he is.	وے هوتے هين	they are.

Perfect.

SINGULAR.		PLURAL.	
مين هوا	I was.	هم هوئے	we were.
تو هوا	thou wast.	تم هوئے	you were.
وه هوا	he was.	وي هوئے	they were.

Preterimperfect.

SINGULAR.			PLURAL.		
هوتا تها	مين	I was.	هوتے تهے	هم	we were.
	تو	thou wast.		تم	you were.
	وه	he was.		وے	they were.

Preterperfect.

SINGULAR.		PLURAL.	
میں هوا هوں	I have been.	هم هوئی هیں	we have been.
تو هوا هي	thou hast been.	تم هوئی هو	you have been.
وه هوا هي	he has been.	وی هوئی هیں	they have been.

Preterpluperfect.

SINGULAR.			PLURAL.		
هوا تها	میں	I had been.	هوئی تهے	هم	we had been.
	تو	thou hadst been.		تم	you had been.
	وه	he had been.		وی	they had been.

Future.

SINGULAR.		PLURAL.	
میں هونگا	I shall be.	هم هوینگے	we shall be.
تو هویگا	thou shalt be.	تم هوگے	you shall be.
وه هویگا	he shall be.	وی هوینگے	they shall be.

CONJUNCTIVE or AORIST.

Present.

SINGULAR.		PLURAL.	
میں هوؤں	I be.	هم هووین	we be.
تو هووي	thou beest.	تم هوؤ	you be.
وه هووی	he be.	وی هووین	they be.

Preterimperfect.

SINGULAR.			PLURAL.		
هوتا	میں	I were.	هوتے	هم	we were.
	تو	thou wert.		تم	you were.
	وه	he were.		وی	they were.

Preterperfect.

SINGULAR.		PLURAL.	
میں ھوا ھووں	I may be.	ھم ھوئی ھوویں	we may be.
تو ھوا ھووی	thou mayest be.	تم ھوئی ھوؤ	you may be.
وہ ھوا ھووی	he may be.	وي ھوئی ھوویں	they may be.

Preterpluperfect.

SINGULAR.		PLURAL.	
اگر میں ھوا ھوتا	if I had been.	اگر ھم ھوئی ھوتے	if we had been.
تو ھوا ھوتا	if thou hadst been.	تم ھوئی ھوتے	if you had been.
وہ ھوا ھوتا	if he had been.	وی ھوئی ھوتے	if they had been.

Future.

SINGULAR.		PLURAL.	
میں ھوا ھوؤنگا	I may have been.	ھم ھوئی ھووینگے	we may have been.
تو ھوا ھوویگا	thou mayst have been.	تم ھوئی ھووگے	you may have been.
وہ ھوا ھوویگا	he may have been.	وي ھوئی ھووینگے	they may have been.

Imperative.

SINGULAR.		PLURAL.	
ھوؤں میں	let me be.	ھوویں ھم	let us be.
ھو تو	be thou.	ھوؤ تم	be you.
ھوی وہ	let him be.	ھوویں وی	let them be.

Infinitive.

PRESENT.		PERFECT.		FUTURE.	
ھونا or ھونے	to be	ھوا ھونا	to have been.	ھوا چاھنا	to be about to be.

Participles—Present.

SINGULAR.		PLURAL.	
ھوتا ھوا or ھوتا	being.	ھوی ھوتے or ھوتے	been.

Perfect.

SINGULAR.	PLURAL.
هوا been.	هوی been.

Preterperfect.

SINGULAR AND PLURAL.

هو هوی هوک هوکر هوکرکم having been.

جانا to be, or to go—used in forming the

PASSIVE VOICE.

The passive differs from the active by substituting جاتا and گیا for هوتا and هوا throughout, as—Indicative Present, مین جاتا هون I am, تو جاتا هي thou art, &c.; Perfect, مین گیا I was; Preterimperfect, مین جاتا تها I was; Preterperfect, مین گیا هون I have been; Preterpluperfect, مین گیا تها I had been; Future, مین جاونگا I shall or may be; Conjunctive or Aorist Present مین جاون I be; Preterimperfect مین جاتا I were; Preterperfect مین جایا جاون I had been; Preterpluperfect مین جایا جاتا I had been; Future مین جایا جاونگا I shall or may have been; Imperative جاون مین let me be; Infinitive Present جانا to be; Perfect جایا جانا to have been; Future جایا چاهنا to be about to be; Participles, Present جاتا or جایا جاتا being; Perfect گیا or گیا هوا been; Preterperfect جا جاي جاکے جاکر جاکرکے having been.

As most verbs in this language are regular, an example of one, Active and Passive, will be sufficient.

سننا to hear.

ACTIVE VOICE.

Indicative Present.

SINGULAR.		PLURAL.	
مین سنتا هون	I hear.	هم سنتے هین	we hear.
تو سنتا هي	thou hearest.	تم سنتے هو	you hear.
وه سنتا هي	he hears.	وي سنتے هین	they hear.

Perfect.

SINGULAR.		PLURAL.	
میں سنا	I heard.	ہم سنے	we heard.
تو سنا	thou heardst.	تم سنے	you heard.
وہ سنا	he heard.	وی سنے	they heard.

Preterimperfect.

SINGULAR.			PLURAL.		
سنتا تھا	میں	I did hear.	سنتے تھے	ہم	we did hear
	تو	thou didst hear.		تم	you did hear.
	وہ	he did hear.		وی	they did hear.

Preterperfect.

SINGULAR.			PLURAL.		
سنا تھا	میں	I have heard.	سنے تھے	ہم	we have heard.
	تو	thou hast heard.		تم	you have heard.
	وہ	he has heard.		وی	they have heard.

Preterpluperfect.

SINGULAR.		PLURAL.	
میں سنا ہوں	I had heard.	ہم سنے ہیں	we had heard.
تو سنا ہے	thou hadst heard.	تم سنے ہو	you had heard.
وہ سنا ہے	he had heard.	وی سنے ہیں	they had heard.

First Future.

SINGULAR.		PLURAL.	
میں سنونگا	I shall hear.	ہم سنینگے	we shall hear.
تو سنیگا	thou shalt hear.	تم سنوگے	you shall hear.
وہ سنیگا	he shall hear.	وی سنینگے	they shall hear.

Second Future.

SINGULAR.		PLURAL.	
میں سنا چاهتا هوں	I will hear.	هم سنے چاهتے هیں	we will hear.
تو سنا چاهتا هي	thou wilt hear.	تم سنے چاهتے هو	you will hear.
وه سنا چاهتا هي	he will hear.	وی سنے چاهتے هیں	they will hear.

CONJUNCTIVE or AORIST.

Present.

SINGULAR.		PLURAL.	
میں سنوں	I may hear.	هم سنیں	we may hear.
تو سنے	thou mayst hear.	تم سنو	you may hear.
وه سنے	he may hear.	وی سنیں	they may hear.

Preterimperfect.

SINGULAR.		PLURAL.	
میں سنتا	I might hear.	هم سنتے	we might hear.
تو سنتا	thou mightst hear.	تم سنتے	you might hear.
وه سنتا	he might hear.	وی سنتے	they might hear.

Preterperfect.

SINGULAR.		PLURAL.	
میں سنا هوؤں	I may have heard.	هم سنے هوویں	we may have heard.
تو سنا هووی	thou mayst have heard.	تم سنے هوؤ	you may have heard.
وه سنا هووی	he may have heard.	وی سنے هوویں	they may have heard.

Preterpluperfect.

SINGULAR.		PLURAL.	
اگر میں } سنا هوتا	if I had heard.	اگر هم } سنے هوتے	if we had heard.
اگر تو } سنا هوتا	if thou hadst heard.	اگر تم } سنے هوتے	if you had heard.
اگر وه } سنا هوتا	if he had heard.	اگر وی } سنے هوتے	if they had heard.

Future.

SINGULAR.		PLURAL.	
میں سنا ہوؤنگا	I should have heard.	ہم سنے ہووینگے	we should have heard.
تو سنا ہوویگا	thou shouldst, &c.	تم سنے ہوؤگے	you should, &c.
وہ سنا ہوویگا	he should, &c.	وے سنے ہووینگے	they should, &c.

Imperative.

SINGULAR.		PLURAL.	
سنوں میں	let me hear.	سنیں ہم	let us hear.
سن تو	hear thou.	سنو تم	hear you.
سنے وہ	let him hear.	سنیں وے	let them hear.

Respectful Imperative.

آپ or صاحب
سنیي or سنییگا } you, or sir, be pleased to hear.

Infinitive.

PRESENT.	PERFECT.	FUTURE.
سننا or سننے to hear.	سنا ہونا to have heard.	سننا چاہنا to be about to hear.

Participles.

PRESENT.		PERFECT.	
سنتا or سنتا ہوا	hearing.	سنا or سنا ہوا	heard.

Preterperfect.

سن سنے سنکے سنکر or سنکرکے having heard.

PASSIVE VOICE.

سنا جانا to be heard.

Indicative.—Present.

میں سنا جاتا ہوں	I am heard.	ہم سنے جاتے ہیں	we are heard.
تو سنا جاتا ہي	thou art heard.	تم سنے جاتے ہو	you are heard.
وہ سنا جاتاہي	he is heard.	وے سنے جاتے ہیں	they are heard.

Perfect.

SINGULAR.			PLURAL.		
سنا گیا	میں	I was heard.	سنے گئے	هم	we were heard.
	تو	thou wast heard.		تم	you were heard.
	وہ	he was heard.		وی	they were heard.

Preterimperfect.

SINGULAR.			PLURAL.		
سنا جاتا تھا	میں	I was heard.	سنے جاتے تھے	هم	we were heard.
	تو	thou wast heard.		تم	you were heard.
	وہ	he was heard.		وی	they were heard.

Preterperfect.

SINGULAR.		PLURAL.	
میں سنا گیا هوں	I have been heard.	هم سنے گئے هیں	we have been heard.
تو سنا گیا هي	thou hast been heard.	تم سنے گئے هو	you have been heard.
وہ سنا گیا هي	he has been heard.	وی سنے گئے هیں	they have been heard.

Preterpluperfect.

SINGULAR.			PLURAL.		
سنا گیا تھا	میں	I had been heard.	سنے گئے تھے	هم	we had been heard.
	تو	thou hadst been heard		تم	you had been heard.
	وہ	he had been heard.		وی	they had been heard.

First Future.

SINGULAR.		PLURAL.	
میں سنا جاونگا	I shall be heard.	هم سنے جاوینگے	we shall be heard.
تو سنا جاویگا	thou shalt be heard.	تم سنے جاؤگے	you shall be heard.
وہ سنا جاویگا	he shall be heard.	وی سنے جاوینگے	they shall be heard.

Second Future.

SINGULAR.		PLURAL.	
میں سنا جایا چاهتا هوں	I will be heard.	هم سنے جائے چاهتے هیں	we will, &c.
تو سنا جایا چاهتا هے	thou wilt, &c.	تم سنے جائے چاهتے هو	you will, &c.
وه سنا جایا چاهتا هے	he will, &c.	وے سنے جائے چاهتے هیں	they will &c.

CONJUNCTIVE or AORIST.

Present.

SINGULAR.		PLURAL.	
میں سنا جاؤں	I may be heard.	هم سنے جاویں	we may be heard.
تو سنا جاوے	thou mayst be heard.	تم سنے جاؤ	you may be heard.
وه سنا جاوے	he may be heard.	وے سنے جاویں	they may be heard.

Preterperfect.

SINGULAR.			PLURAL.		
سنا جاتا	اگر میں	if I were heard.	سنے جاتے	اگر هم	if we were heard.
	اگر تو	if thou wert heard.		اگر تم	if you were, &c.
	اگر وه	if he were heard.		اگر وے	if they were, &c.

Preterpluperfect.

SINGULAR.	سنا جایا جاتا	اگر میں	if I had been heard.
		اگر تو	if thou hadst been heard.
		اگر وه	if he had been heard.
PLURAL.	سنے جائے جاتے	اگر هم	if we had been heard.
		اگر تم	if you had been heard.
		اگر وے	if they had been heard.

Future.

SINGULAR.	مین سنا جایا جاؤنگا	I shall have been heard.
	تو سنا جایا جاویگا	thou shall have been heard.
	وہ سنا جایا جاویگا	he shall have been heard.
PLURAL.	هم سنے جاے جاوینگے	we shall have been heard.
	تم سنے جاے جاؤگے	you shall have been heard.
	وے سنے جاے جاوینگے	they shall have been heard.

Imperative.

SINGULAR.		PLURAL.	
سنا جاؤن مین	let me be heard.	سنے جاوین هم	let us be heard.
سنا جاوے تو	be thou heard.	سنے جاؤ تم	be you heard.
سنا جاوے وہ	let him be heard.	سنے جاوین وے	let them be heard.

Infinitive.

PRESENT. سنا جانا to be heard. PERFECT. سنا جایا جانا to have been, &c.

FUTURE. سنا جایا چاهنا to be about to be heard.

Participles.

PRESENT. سنا جاتا being heard. PERFECT. سنا گیا heard.

PRETERPERFECT.

سنا جایا جا جاے جاکر or جاکرکے having been heard.

The final ا of the infinitive and participles is changed into ي in the feminine singular, and ين or يان in the plural; and by the same rule, those tenses that have final ا in the singular masculine, change that letter into ي in the feminine, as مین سنتا هون I (male) hear, مین سنتي هون I (female) hear, &c.

NEGATIVE VERBS.

These Verbs are formed by prefixing نه or نهين through all the persons and tenses, except the imperative, which takes مت in some of the persons, as—مين نهين سنتا هون I do not hear, تو نه سنتا تها thou didst not hear, وه نسنے let him not hear, هم نهين سنينگے we will not hear, تم مت سنو do not hear, وي مت سنين let them not hear.

IRREGULAR VERBS.

There are very few Irregular Verbs in this language, and those only in what is termed the perfect tense; as كرنا to make, كيا made, مرنا to die, مرا or موا died, دينا *dena* to give, ديا *dee-a* he gave, لينا *lena* to take, ليا *leea* he took, هونا *hona* to be, هوا *hooa* been, was, جانا to go, to be, گيا went, was.

TRANSITIVE VERBS.

These are formed by inserting ا *a* or وا *wa* before, نا *na* of the infinitive, as بهرنا to fill, بهرانا to cause to fill, كرنا to make, كرانا to cause to make, گانا to sing, گاوانا to cause to sing. Those, as well as intransitives, often take the particle نے *ne* after the pronoun, which serves to simplify the conjugation, and to confine it to the nominative case, there being no change of persons, singular or plural in the tenses in which it is used; and, the third person singular and plural, are expressed by اس and ان instead of وه and وي as—

گاوايا	مين نے I caused to sing.		گاوايا	هم نے we caused to sing.
	تو نے thou causedst to sing.			تم نے you caused to &c.
	اس نے he caused to sing.			ان نے they caused, &c.

Preterperfect مين نے گوايا هي I have caused to sing, تونے گوايا هي thou hast caused to sing, &c.; preterpluperfect مين نے گوايا تها I had caused to sing; future مين نے گوايا هوگا I shall cause to sing; conjunctive preterperfect مين نے گوايا هووي I may have caused to sing, &c.

When the vowel of the root is long it is shortened before the affixes ا and وا, as ڈوبنا to be drowned, ڈبونا or ڈبانا to cause to be drowned; and when the root ends in a long vowel, the letter ل is generally inserted in the transitive, and the vowel becomes a short one, as پينا to drink, پلوانا to cause to drink; and sometimes ا follows ل as سيکهنا to learn, سِکهلانا to cause to learn, to teach.

COMPOUND VERBS.

This class consists of two verbs joined together as ڈال دينا to throw away from, ڈالنا to throw, and دينا to give, دی ڈالنا to give away, گر پڑنا to fall, پکڑ پانا to find out, نکال دينا to throw out, to reject, بجهجانا to go out, اوتر پڑنا to alight.

Some are formed of Persian or Arabic nouns and the auxiliary verbs کرنا دينا لينا &c. as درد کرنا to pain, خبر دينا to inform, رخصت لينا to take leave. Others are formed of Persian adjectives and native auxiliaries, as خوش کرنا to please, خوش هونا to rejoice, خوش هوجانا to be pleasant.

The tenses of the potential mood are formed by the auxiliary سکنا to be able, which is conjugated regularly, like other verbs, as مين سکتا هون I can, مين سکا I could, مين سکونگا I shall be able, &c. مين سن سکونگا I shall be able to hear, &c.

TO HAVE.

The verb *to have* is expressed, as in Latin and Arabic, by هونا to be, with a dative case, as مجهے ايک دوست هي I have a friend, مجهے ايک دوست تها I had a friend, مجهے ايک دوست هوگا I shall have a friend, مجهے بهت يارون هين I have many friends, &c.

FORMATION of DERIVATIVES.

Names of agents, &c. are formed by adding هارا اک والا and other particles to nouns, verbal roots, and inflected infinitives, as—

دده milk, ددهوالا a milkman, ددهوالي a milkmaid, دوڑ run, دوڑاک a runner, لکهنا to write, لکنیوّالا a writer, دیو a God, دیوستهان a temple, کهیل play, کهیلار a player, لوت plunder, لوٹیڑا a plunderer, هنس laugh, هنسوڑا a laugher, ڈک a blow, ڈکیت a robber, کود jump, کودکر a jumper, چڑا a bird, چڑي مار a bird-catcher, هندو an Hindoo, هندوپت a lord of the Hindoos, بن a forest, بن واري a forester, جي life, جي نگر the city of life, علي Ali, علي پور the town of Ali, رام Ram, رام گڑه the fort of Ram, لون salt, لون گولا a salt market, نام a name, نام مالا a book of names, راگ مالا a song book, پڑها read, انپڑها illiterate, بیاه marriage, بیاه جوگ marriageable, بنس a bamboo, بنس باڑي a plantation of bamboos, دهرم alms, دهرم سالا an alms house, بیج seed, بیجالا seedy, پتهر a stone, پتهریلا stony, بڑا great, بڑاپا grandeur, لڑکا a child, لڑکاپن childhood, کڑوا bitter, کڑواهت bitterness, بنا prepared, بناوت management, دبا chiding, دباؤ authority, کهیت a field, کهیتوا a little field, بل power, بلونت powerful, لڑا causing to fight, لڑاک quarrelsome, بده wisdom, بدهمان intelligent, بهادر brave, بهادري bravery, چتر sly چترائي slyness, سجا cause to prepare, سجاو preparation.

Words borrowed from the Persian and Arabic generally form their derivatives conformably to the rules of those languages, as—

زر gold, زرگر a goldsmith, نگه a look, نگهبان an observer, تیر an arrow, تیر زن an archer, شیر a lion, شیرستان a country abounding with lions, لاله a tulip, لاله زار a tulip bed, نمک salt, نمک دان a saltcellar, خواب sleep, خوابگاه a bed, دست a hand, دسته a handle, انگشت a finger, انگشتونه a thimble, کنیز a girl, کنیزک a little girl, باغ a garden, باغچه a little garden, سیم silver, سیمین silvery, مرد a man, مردانه manly, نقل a narrative, نقل بند an historian, دانش wisdom, دانشمند wise, مال wealth, مالدار wealthy, شرم shame, شرمسار bashful, غم sorrow, غمگين sorrowful, خشم anger, خشمناک angry, اميد hope, اميدوار hopeful, جان life, جانور a living creature, دل a heart, دل آور a ravisher of hearts, پري an angel, پريزاد born of an angel, زمرد an emerald, زمرد نام of an emerald colour, گل a rose, گلفام of the colour of roses, پنج five, پنجگوشه a pentagon, پاک pure, ناپاک impure, شي a thing, لاشي nothing, باک fear, بي باک fearless.

From the Arabic root قبل he received, the following derivatives are formed:—قابل receiving, مقبول accepted, اقبال prosperity, اقبالاً prosperously, تقبيل accepting, تقابل encountering, تقبيل embracing, قبلة a charming woman, قبول consenting, قبولي acceptable, قبوليّت reception, قبيل capable, قبيلاً a little before, مقتبل one in the bloom of youth, مقبول approaching, مقبّل a person or place kissed, متقابل opposed, استقبال going to meet.

Arabic and Persian words often take the following particles, prefixed or separate, ال the به با ب with, in, to, بي without, از from, بر upon, براي for, بعد after, در in, در ميان among, سوا besides, علي according to, عن concerning, عند near, في in, ک like, ل to, مع with, من from.

NUMERALS.

ايک one, دو two, تين three, چار four, پانچ five, چهه six, سات seven, آتهه eight, نو nine, دس ten, اگاره eleven, باره twelve, تيره thirteen, چوده fourteen, پندره fifteen, سوله sixteen, ستره seventeen اتهاره eighteen, انيس nineteen, بيس twenty, اکيس twenty-one, بايس twenty-two, تيئيس twenty-three, چوبيس twenty-four, پچيس twenty-five, چهبيس twenty-six, ستائيس twenty-seven, اتهائيس twenty-eight, انتيس twenty-nine, تيس thirty, اکتيس thirty-one, &c. چاليس forty, پچاس fifty, ساتهه sixty, ستر seventy, اسي eighty, نوے ninety, سي or سو one hundred, ايک سو ايک one hundred and one.

INDECLINABLES.

اندر within, بیچ in, among, پاس near, at, کنے near, with, ساتھ along with, آگے in front, سامھنے in the presence, بھاوین in choice, باھر on the outside, اوپر upon, نیچے under, تلے below, پار over, across, مارے for, لییے on account, واستے for, یہاں here, ھاتھ at hand, اب now, تلک or تک to, until توڑي till, لگ to, until اب تب presently, اب تک till now, کب تک till when, کبھي ever, کبھي کبھي sometimes, کب سے since when, کب لو till when, کبھي نہین never, جب when, جب تک till when, جب کبھي whenever, جب کا تب at the proper moment, جب نہ تب perpetually, تب تلک till then, یہیں in this place, یہان تک hithertو, وھاں there, وھیں yonder, جہان where, جہاں جہاں wherever جہاں تہاں wherever, جہاں کہیں wherever, کہاں where, تہاں there, کہیں somewhere, کہیں نہ کہیں somewhere or other, کہیں نہیں no where, ھر کہیں every where, اَور کہیں elsewhere, اِدھر or ایدھر here, hither, اُدھر or اودھر there, thither, کِدھر or کیدھر where? whither? جِدھر or جیدھر where, whither, تدھر or تیدھر there, thither, کِدھر سے whence, جِدھر تِدھر here and there, یون thus, یون نہ یون one way or other, وون in that manner, وون کا وون as before, وونہیں just then, کیون or کیونکر why? how? جیون or جیونکر as, like, تیون or تیونکر so, thus, جیون جیون whenever, تیون تیون so, at that time, جیون کا تیون just the same, جیون تیون some how or other, جو نہیں just when, ایسا thus, ویسا so, کیسا how? تیسا so, جیسا as, جیسا تیسا as well as, ایتنا thus much, اُتنا that much, کتنا how much, جتنا as much as, تتنا so much تي بیر so often, جي بیر as often, کي بیر how often, اتیبار frequently, پھر or پُن again, ترت or ترنت instantly, چٹ or جھٹ quickly, امنے سامنے face to face, سنمکھ opposite, سنگ with, بسمیت along with, پي nevertheless, نیرے beside, near, سینت gratis, اَچت unaware, پہلا before, پہلے in the first place, دوسرے in the second place, ندان at last, آج to day, کل yesterday, or tomorrow, آج کل now a-days, پرسون two days ago or to come, ترسون three days, &c. نرسون four days, &c. تڑکے at dawn of day, سبیرے in the morning.

هان yes, نهین or نه no.

CONJUNCTIONS, &c. borrowed from the Arabic and Persian.

و and, هم also, بلکه but, لیکن but, اما but, یا or پس then, نیز also, ور *for* و اگر and if, ورنه unless, اگرچه although, حال آنکه whereas, بنابرین therefore, زیرا because, هرچندکه although. یعني that is, گویا thus, همیشه always, مدام perpetually, هرگز ever, گاه گاهي at some time, هنوز yet, چنانچه as, like, الا unless, حسب accordingly, غیر besides, وغیره et cetera, مثلاً for example, خصوصاً particularly, دفعتاً often, عقلاً prudently, قبلاً cordially—

SYNTAX.

The Hindoostanee has its poetic licenses like other languages; and its construction is so pliable, that it will admit of a variety of forms without injury to the sense. The adjective, in poetry, may be placed either before or after the noun as most suitable to the metre; but in prose it is for the most part placed before it. Nouns of different genders, joined together, require the adjective, participle, &c. by which they are governed to be masculine. Personal pronouns are frequently omitted, when understood; and when expressed, they generally precede the verb. The first person singular is commonly used in the plural, even by people of the lowest *caste*, as هم سنتے هین we hear, *for* مین سنتا هون I hear: and in order to distinguish the real plural, they are obliged to have recourse to the words لک people, سب all, &c. as هم لک سنتے هین we people hear. The second person plural is generally used as with us, in speaking respectfully to any one, and the third person plural in speaking of a third person. In repeating any thing spoken by a third person, the third person is commonly changed to the first, as اس نے کہا کہ میں آ سکونگا he says he shall be able to come; *literally*, he said, I shall be able to come.— The verb usually follows its noun or nouns, closes the sentence, and accords with its subject in gender, number, and person; but sometimes a singular nominative is used with a plural in respect to a superior, and sometimes a verb is adopted in the singular with a noun in the plural number. When the particle نے occurs, کو is omitted, and the dative or accusative takes a nominative form. Compound verbs frequently take کا کے or کي and sometimes کو in the oblique, as اِس بات کا فکر کرو think of this matter, اِس بات کو غور کرتا هي he studies this business. The infinitive is often used as a gerund or verbal noun, and sometimes as a noun of instrument; it is declined like nouns, and changes نا into نے in the oblique, as اِس بات کو فکر کرنے لگا he began to study this affair. The participle present denotes immediate action, as وہ دوڑتے ھوے on his running, the perfect what has transpired, as جسکے سنے, which having heard, but the preterperfect سنکر is more common.

Prepositions, follow the oblique of verbal and declinable nouns when they are not joined to numerals, consequently, they are termed postpositions. The particles آگے اوپر پاس &c. are used with inflected nouns and require the genitive sign کا کے or کي either expressed or understood. The words اگر and جو *if* require پس or تو *then*, to follow in the sentence. جُوں and جیوں are answered by تیوں or توں as is جوں جوں by توں توں—اور or او *and* are often omitted in Hindoostanee when indispensable in English, as لڑکا لڑکي a boy (and) girl. Sometimes words are doubled in order to vary the meaning, as پانچ پانچ five five, for five or six, or a few, ایک ایک one by one, singly, دیکھ دیکھ continuing to look, anxious, دیکھا دیکھي competition, دیکھا دیکھایا already seen, دیکھا نہ دیکھا whether seen or not.

Having laid down within a small compas all that is essential to hindoostanee grammar, I now proceed to give a few pages from original manuscripts for the exercise of the student.

Some attempts have been made by modern moonshies (for the use of europeans) to distinguish the sounds of certain letters, viz. ھ for the aspirated letters borrowed from the Sanscrit, as ख घ &c, and ہ for the common *h*, as کھا *he ate*, کہا *he said*. They have established it as a rule, that ي with points sounds *ee*, and without so, ی ے long *e*; ن with a point as the common *n*; without a point as nazal *n*; ک as common *k*; with a dash above, so گ, as our hard *g*. These niceties however, are not much, if at all, observed by the natives, whose best manuscripts are written without any such discriminations, as may be seen in the succeeding pages which have been copied with care as regards the letters above mentioned, in order to afford persons unprovided with manuscripts an opportunity of familiarizing themselves with the native writings.

کہانی اول

اوّل کي دور میں ایك بادشاد تھا مشہور او جون سورماہ تھا
سرندیب مین اتھا او بخت وراج قدم آدمکا اوسکے سیس کا تاج
اتھا عاقل چتر پر دیت دانی نتھا دنیا میں اوسکا کوئی ثاني
ھنر جسمین دیسے دانش وریکا اوسے منصب دلاوی سروریکا
عجب خوبیکا دلمین رنگ رس تھا بزرکان سات ملنے کا ھوس تھا
اتھے اس شاھکون سب تین فرزند یکس تھي ایك عاقل سب خردمند
ادک رستم سون او ھر یک کھاتے اتھي شررزي ھتے جون کیند اوچاتے
تونکر علم ھور تھي مال دھن مین نتھی عاجز ھر یک حکمت کے فنمین
سکل عاقل اننکي جون قلے تھے که جون دانا فلاطون بوعلي تھے
تجانون کیا نول شاہ دلمین لایا حدا ھر یک جوانکون شاہ بولایا

کہیا ہر یک جوانکون ازمانا　جو ہي کل جوک کا کہوتا زمانا

دہرونکا کون کہتا ہي سپاہي　کرونکا کون کہتا پادشاہي

بری فرزند کون بولا اي ہنرمند　کہ تون عاقل سنجے عادل خرد مند

کہتے جا عمر کا کنچن ہوا صرف　ہوا جنکل جواني کیس جون برف

جواني لي دیا جق مجکون پیري　خدا تجکون کیا ہي دستکیري

بہونت عاقل ہي کرنون پادشاہي　سکل خوبي سون رکہنا مرغ و ماہي

جو راضي جم اچہي معبود تجہ سون　ضعیفان کون کري تعظیم سب سون

ضعیفانکون بہونت کر دستکیري　جوکوي دانا ہي اوسکون دی امیری

جتن کر باک سون نہ کري سجاني　ندی تون کرک کون اوسکا شباني

دہریا سر بہوین کہیا دانا خردمند　بہادر پادشاہ نیک فرزند

جدہان لک ہین ککن پرچاندتاري　جدہان لک عرش کرسي ہي جماري

تدہان لک کرتون جکمین بادشاہي　اچہي تجہ شاہ عالم کي سیاہي

چرین کر تخت اوپر مرغ و ماهي سلیمان کا نکر سے پادشاهي

عجب تون تخت افسر بخت هوشیار بغیر از تجه نهین کسکو سرافراز

تونکر کون نکهسے بینوا کون ندیسے پادشادي کویي کدا کون

اکر نادان کون جینے سون کام هي بغیر دانا اوسي جینا حرام هي

جهلکتاهي جهان ملك تجه سارکا نور ستاري تیون همین دستے هین بےنور

بهونت جک راج کرتون شادماني خضر کا حم چهو تجه زندکاني

سرا سر آزمایا شاه کفتار کهیا دلمین که هي یو نیك کردار

کیا دلمین خوشي جب آزمایا ولي ظاهر غضب کر بهار بهایا

اتها فرزند دو جا اوس بلایا کتنك دلکي خوشي سون ازمایا

بهونت افسونکري سون دل بهلایا ولي ذره خطا اسمین نه پایا

سوالان جو کیا شاه خردمند جوابانسون کیا فرزند زبان بند

کهیا جوتون کهي سو مین کرونکا تیرا فرمان سریرمین دهرونکا

ولي يو بادشاهي بجه اوا هی   ولي دو جا منکي او نا سازا هي

نهين معلوم باتان غيب کے مجه   تخت کا ناٴون لينا عيب هي مجه

يتا کان زور هي بنديکي دم کون   دهرونکا تخت پر جيو کي قدم کون

فلك بي مهر اکر تجسون پهريکا   کيا دسريانسون او تجه سون کريکا

کياني کون ابد لک زندکاني   وفا کس نين کيا دنياي فاني

اکر هوي کدهين تو شاه راضي   کري يو تخت جکمين سرفرازي

بري فرزند کون دی تخت کياني   تيري بعد از کريکا جلك نوازي

بري بن نا چهڑی معراج پر کوي   نتها موتي نرکهسے تاج پر کوي

نين لي بهار سر کا نا مروسے   بغير از پيٹ بهي کوي پند نہ ليسے

بنديا شه کانت دی دو چاند يکسور   حضوري تها نظر سون اوس کيا دور

کيا شه رنج جدهر تها خورد دانا   کيا جن عقل مين جلك کون ديوانا

لکيا شه بهوت چهند سون ازمانے   کنک جيو کے کسوتي پر لکاني

دیا یون جواب اونے ای شاہ کیانی که طفلانسون نهو ے کاردانی

جب اس فرزند کون شه آزمایا بهوت کچه شادمانی دلمین پایا

کهیا شه تین کوهر هین شرفناک رتن جون کهانکی هین سو رسون پاک

هوا خوشحال اپنی تخت سر سون کیا سجده خدا کون تخت پر سون

طمع کسی مین نهین هی مال دهنکا خبر دهرتی هین نادر هر بچنکا

ولی فرمان دیا تینور تن کون نکل جاؤ تمین هر یک پتن سون

جهانلک هی میوا سب مرغ وماهی جهان پرتی هی مجه شه کی دوراهی

رهینکی وهان تو مارون خوارکر مین سیاست کر دهرونکا دار پر مین

کهی جب بات آشهکی پیا دی سیاه پوش هو چلی او شاه زادی

بندی تو شه چلی ست طمع کهرکا تماشا دیکهتی سب بحر و برکا

کیئ جب شاه زادی شهرسون بهار بغیر جنکل پهاران کوی نتها یار

جو کچه پهر شهر مین آوی سو کهتی خرابی مین که هین جون شیر رهتی

اتھا سب مغز سر مین سروریکا ولی پکری هنر سود اکریکا

هریک شهکي نکرمین یو دلیران چلین بکریان اپرجون مست شیران

هوا یکدن قضای آسمانی چلي یکتهار مل یو یار جانی

جو تل یک شهر کي نزدیک آیي بندی کهري وهان آرام پائیي

اتها اوس شهر کي نزدیگ جنگل رهے اوس بن مین یوجون مست منگل

یکایك یک زنکي دور آیا که جون شیطان اپنا مکه دیکهایا

براتهو بر دیسي چو کرد اسکی مکر شیطان سب سا کرد اسکي

نین زنکي کے جون کاریگي چاکان هتم سب نهاستي سن اسکي هانکان

لهویکي کانمین یک با ولي تهي مثل سے پیت پر روما ولي تهي

ادهر اوپرال کا ناسکه پر آیا ادهر د سرا سوبین بي کون چهپایا

بند یا تها چهارکي چوکرد پانان هتي کي دانت سون کچه کم تهي داتان

اتها بد شکل کالا جون سیا هي دیکهت شیطان دری هورموغ و ماهے

اکر کوی اوس بر نکا تل جولا وي   سورج هورد یس کون اوتل چهپاوي

کهیا اي سور بني سور زادي   هریك مین چاند یا هین شاه زادي

میرا یك اونٹ اوس باتون کیا هي   نشاني دیوین تو مجهر میا هي

کیا هي کان اکر بولین تو جاؤن   مهنے کا خبر یك پلمین لیاؤن

کهیا اوس تین مین کا یك خردمند   جو تهي عاقل هنرمند شهکي فرزند

کهیا دانا شترور زور هي او   کهیا ایك آنکه اوسکا کور هي او

کهیا دسرا چتر کهتا دهرم هي   که اوسکے موں منے یك دانت کم هي

کهیا تیزا جو عارف رنك برنك هي   ولي اوس اونٹ کا یك پاؤن لنك هے

دیے هریك جواب اس د هات باتون   کیا هي اونٹ تیرا بیك جاتون

هریك عارف بچن کون جب سنایا   دهوندن هاري کون جا نو جیو آیا

پون تیون مرد کیتا کام کون او   چلیا چون شاطر اپنی کام کون او

هلون دلتے چلي جانا سو بن مین   پون سون چون سرو د لتا چمن مین

چرن کي اوترنک کرتے ننهي کرم   قدم پر دهر قدم چلتي انهي نرم

چلي آئے وهان يون تين کياني   اتها يک باغ نادر صاف پاني

دسيا يک جهاڑ اونچا جون ککن تها   هوا هور چهانسون چوندهر پهولبن تها

برک طوبا مکر تها ناؤن اوسکا   جو يکيک کوس دوريا چهانون اوسکا

کچه کچ کهابي پيبي مکه هات دهوي   بندي کهوري وهان تک سکه سون سوي

هوي هشيار بيتي بات کرتي   خوشي کون ياد کرتي غم بسرتي

کيا سو ساربان بهي پهر کر آيا   بهونت کچه شور هور غوغا اونچايا

غضب کے آگ سون روشن کراکر   زبانکي تيغ کون پاني دلاکر

کيا دس کوس دوريا هون اودهر مين   جهان بولي تمين ديکهيا ادهر مين

کهين ديکهيا هون بيچهو سانپ جهاڑان   کهين ديکهيا هون کانتي سخت ماران

ولي ديکهيا نهين مين کرد اوسکا   بهريا هر بال مين سب درد اوسکا

پون تيون مين بهونت جلدي سون دهايا   اوريا هي کهن اوپريا بهوين چهو پايا

کھیا جانا تمین یک جان دانا　　جوکچھ سمجا هون مین سونا چھپانا

کھرا کھیوؑ کا بھریا هراس طرف جان　　شهد اوس طرف لادیا هي مرد بتان

کھیا دو جاکه اسپرا ستري هي　　چتر باغ ارم کي شاه پري هي

کھیا تیسرا جوهي او پیٹ سون نار　　شکم کی بہار سون هوتا هي آزار

نشانیان تھي جتي پایا او زنکي　　کیا ثابت انن پر او که زنکي

نهین سمجا انن مین هي امیري　　هاون آکر کیا او خورد کیری

کہا یو چورهین دستي بهلي یو　　بشر کي کاٹ تي پهرتي کلے یو

ترنك مانک رتن کسکا چوراوین　　اوجون سرمه نین میاني چھپاوین

میتي بانان سون کرتي دل نوازي　　تمرپن تهي تمن دیتي هین بازي

کہرانمین کهان بهاتي هو سنا سے　　جنکل مین خاق کون دیتي هین پهانسے

بری ساحر پري هین چور سر زور　　چور امردا کفن خالي کرین کور

زبانکا کرد هند وراشور اوچایا　　تماشا دیکهني سب حلق دهایا

ملي هالي نمن سب خلق ساري   اتهي جون چاند يو مياني بچاري

رکتے کهتي او تهي يو شاه زادي   رکتے کهتي اهين يو چور پيادي

کهي سب مل که تينونکون جکر کر   ليجا تون شه کني سبکون پکر کر

جب آيي شه کني تينون جوانان   نظر کر خوب ديکها شاه دانا

کهيا تو ساربان سب کن کي دهاتان   نشانيان اونٹ کي بولي سوبايان

سکل باتان نول شاه کن کهيا او   جتا کهتا اتها که چپ رهيا او

کهيا تينونکون شه يو حال کيا هي   کهو اسبات کا احوال کيا هي

دعا اول کييۓ او تين ياران   جو اپني ملك کي تهي تاجداران

جدان لك رات دن هي مرغ و ماهے   تدهانلك کر تون جکمين پادشاهي

جدهانلك هي دهرت پرسورکا نور   اچهو تجه شاه کا يو ملك معمور

همين تينو مسافر هين غريبان   جهانکي فيض سون هين بي نصيبان

بهونت شد تسون پهرتي هين اودا سي   رياضت کا کلي مين ڈال پهان سی

همین دیکھي تماشا سب نکر کا   عجایب ہور غرایب بحر و بر کا

ولي دیکھي خدا کي بھونت پاکان   جنکل دیکھی پہاران ہوو مغاکان

نھین همناکون بھاتا شہر کوشا   طمع کانین هماري پاس توشا

خدا کا ھي بھونت همنا پہ سایا   جو شہکي شہر کي نزدیک لایا

اول ایا یو زنکي جون سپاھي   دري جنکل کي ساري مرغ و ماھي

نھیا دیکھین میرا اونٹ بولو   دریچي راستي کي خوب کھولو

ظرافتکا او رائیي باتسون زاغ   کھي ھنسنی لکیا بد نام کا داغ

کناہ کي تول کي همناکون جھولي   نھین دیکھي سوباتان جھوت بولي

غضب مین اکھیا تو شاہ کیاني   نھین دیکھي سو بولي کیون نشاني

ستي ھین دل سون باھر راز کي تیر   پھر اسے نا بھاني کا یو تد بیر

لیا سودی نچل سے کچھ بھانا   نکون کر تدیر کا دلکون نشانا

کھیا شہ ھین دغاباز یو ستمکار   لیجا کر بند کرو یو ھین کناہ کار

هوا تها نس چهپا سورج ككن مين   كه جون يونس چهپے ماهي كے تن مين

چلي زندان طرف ياران جاني   وفا كس نين كيا دنياي فاني

رهي سب نس ككن مين جون ستاري   نمر چوران حراميانمين بچاري

ديا سورج كون اپنا ماه شاهي   هوا هشيار تب سب مرغ و ماهي

هوا جب مكه نوراني سب جهانكا   كيا جو اونت تها اوس ساربانكا

نجانون كان كيا تها بحر و بر هين   چليا آيا شتر بانكي او كهر مين

صنم میرا سخن سون آشنا هي   مجهي فکر سخن کرنان بجا هي

چمن مین حسن کي هر جلوۂ یار   گل رنگین بهار مدعا هي

نه بخشي کیون تیرا خط زندکاني   که موج چشمۂ آب بقا هي

تغافل نین تیري زخمي کیا مجهه   تیري بوکم نکا هي بیم جا هي

وهي اوی هي راه عشقي مین   که جسکون استقامت کا عصا هي

نهین هي آب غیر از آب خنجر   شهادت کاه عاشق کر بلا هي

غنیمت بوجه ملني کون ولي کي
نکاه پاکباز ان کیمیا هي

کمر اس دلربا کي دلربا هي   نکه اوس خوش ادا کي آدا هي

یو خط هي جوهو آیینه پرداز   اسي مشک ختن کهتان بجا هي

هوا معلوم تجهه زلفان سرن اي سوخ   که شاه حسن پرظل هما هي

نه هووی کوهکن کیون اي عاشق   که وو شیرین آدا کلکون قبا هي

نہ پوچھو آہ و زاری کي حقیقت عزیزان عاشقان کا مقتضا هے

ولي کون ست ملامت کراي واعظ

ملامت عاشقان پر کب روا هي

گلستان لطافت کا تیرا قد سرو رعنا هي

همیشه نازکي آب جو مین جلوه سراهي

هوا هي دلنشین وو سرو قامت بسکه مجهه دلمین

قد سرو کر میري سایه سون پیدا هو تو بر جا هي

پریشاني کے مکتب کا معلم اسکون کهه سکي

تیري زلف پریشان کا صنم جس سر مین سودا هي

ولي میري تواضع سون رقیب سنگدل دایم

پشیمان هي خجل هي منفعل مي سخت رسوا هي

The former of the above specimens is taken from the قصۂ بہرام هفت حکایت or seven tales of Beheram Goor, a work founded upon Nizámi's poem of هفت پیکر *heft peeker* or the seven faces; the latter is from the دیوان ولی *divâni Wali* or odes of Wuli, much admired in India. The hindoostanee tongue so abounds in persian words and phrases, that a person who has acquired a moderate knowledge of the persian poets, might in a very short time become familiar with those of the hindoostanee; and even in prose it is evident that a close connexion subsists between the two languages. I have selected a few tales &c, from the persian Tooti-nameh, and Gulistan, and, to shew the great affinity these languages bear to each other, I have given the corresponding translations of Meer Sher Ulee Ufsos, into the hindoostanee.

The translation of the Gulistan, it appears, was undertaken "For the use of the students at the college of Fort William, under the direction and superintendence of John Gilchrist, &c. Printed at Calcutta 1802." The type used in this book is an imitation of the taaleek character, which, being more difficult to read than the plain niskhy character, these selections may be found useful to the young orientalist by enabling him to compare the characters of the Calcutta edition with the plain ones of this work. The Tooti-nameh and the Gulistan were translated into english by the late Mr Gladwin, to whose researches in oriental literature, the public are highly indebted.

SELECTIONS.

PERSIAN AND HINDOOSTANEE.

PERSIAN.

TALE CONSTRUED, FROM THE TOOTI NAMEH.

شیر و برهمن که طمع کرده جان خود داد

The Lion and the Brahmin, who, on account of his avarice, lost his life.

چون آفتاب غروب شد و ماه آمد خجسته بطلب رخصت بر طوطي

When / the sun / set / was / and / the moon / risen, / Khojisteh / for / leave / to / the parrot

رفت و گفت که میدانم که ترا از درد من خبر نیست از ین سبب

went, / and / said / I am / sensible / that / yourself / about / the / uneasi- / ness / of me / you / trouble / not, / on / that / account

مرا رخصت نمیکني و حکایات درمیان مي آري طوطي گفت اي

me / dispatch / you do / not, / but / tales / in- / troduce. / The / parrot / said, / O

خجسته از خدا مي خواهم که تو جلد تر بمعشوق خود برسي تو خود

Khojisteh / to / God / I wish / that / you / speedily / to your / lover / would go; / you / yourself

توقف میکني تقصیر من هیچ نیست امشب جلد برو لیکن باید که

the delay / make / the fault / of me / it is not. / To-night / quickly / go; / but / you must

HINDOOSTANEE.

ایک برهمن نے لالچ کو کام فرمایا اور شیر کے هاتهه سے مارا گیا

جب سورج چهپا اور سانجهه هویے خجسته بیقراروں کے سے صورت بنایے هوئی توتي کي پاس رخصت لینے گیی اور کهنے لگي اي توتي معلوم هوا تجهي میری درد کي خبر نهیں جب هي میری باتیں اڑا دیتا هي اور ادهر ادهر کي جهوتهه سچ قصي اور کهانیاں سنایا کرتا هي نهیں جانتي که تجهي اس سے کیا حاصل هي • توتي نے کها اي گدبانو میں خدا سے چاهتا هوں که تو جلد کهیں اس کے پاس جاوي اور اسے گلي لگاوي توآپ هي نهیں جاتي اور دیر کرتي هي اس میں میری تقصیر کچهه نهیں

یوں آپ کي خوشي هي مجهي قتل کیجیي • پر حق تو هي یهي که میری کچهه خطا نهیں • خیر اب شتاب جا اور اس سے ملاقات کرکي

When the sun was set, and the moon risen, Khojisteh went to the parrot for leave, and said, "I am sensible you do not trouble yourself about my uneasiness, and on that account do not dispatch me, but introduce tales." The parrot said, "I wish to God, Khojisteh, that you would go speedily to your lover! you yourself make the delay; it is no fault of mine. Go quickly, to-night; but you must

جلد مراجعت کني و در آنجا هيچ طمع نه نمايي زيرا که طمع نمودن

soon | return, | and | there | any thing | covet | do not, | for | inordinate | desire

بسيار بد است و هرکه طمع نمود همان ديد که برهمن ديد خجسته

is sinful | and | whosoever | is avari- | cious | the same | fate | will meet | with | as the | brahmin. | Khojisteh

پرسيد که حکايت آن چگونه است بگو

said | The story | of that | what | is? | Tell (me).

طوطي آغاز کرد که در شهري برهمني بود مالدار اتفاقاً مفلس گرديد

The parrot | began, | In | a certain | city | a Brahmin | was | rich, | who | happening | poor | to become

لاچار بسفر رفت روزي در بياباني رسيد و ديد که شيري بر کنارهٔ تالاب

and destitute, | a journey | went; | one day | in | a desert | he arrived | and | saw | a lion | by | the side of | a pond

غلتيده است و روباه و آهو پيش او استاده برهمن متفکر گرديد و

wollowing | with | a fox | and | a deer | be fore | him | standing. | The | Brahmin | con- | founded | and

ترسان استاده شد ناگاه نظر آهو و روباه بر برهمن افتاد آنها با يکديگر

dreading | stood. | Suddenly, | the sight | of the deer | and | the fox | on | the | brahmin | fell; | they | to | one | another

گفتند که اگر شير خواهد ديد اين بيچاره مسکين را خواهد کشت

said, | if | the lion | should | see, | this | helpless | poor | fellow | he will | kill;

جلد پهیر آ پر یہہ یاد رکهه که وهاں کسي چیز کي طمع نه کرنا کیونکه، لالچ بہت بڑي بلا هي اگر طمع کریگي تو تیرا بہي حال ویسا هي هوگا جیسا که اس برهمن کا هوا تها خجسته نے پوچها اس کي نقل کیونکر هي

توتا کہنے لگا کسي شهر میں ایک برهمن نہایت مالدار تها اتفاقاً وہ مفلس هوکر اور کسي ملک میں کچهه پیدا کرنے چلا . ناگاه ایک روز کسي جنگل میں جا پہنچا اور تالاب کي کناري پر دیکها که ایک شیر بیتها هي ایک لومڑي اور هرني اس کي آگي کهڑي هي . یہه برهمن متفکر هوکر ڈرکی ماری وونہیں کهڑا هورها که یکایک لومڑي کي اور هرني کي نظر اس پر جا پڑی تب آپس میں سوچ کر یوں بولیاں که اگر اس کو شیر دیکهیگا تو مار هي ڈالیگا

soon return, and do not covet any thing that is there, for inordinate desire is sinful, and whosoever is avaricious, will meet with the same fate as the Brahmin." Khojisteh said, Tell me what is that story?

The parrot began, "In a certain city was a rich Brahmin, who happening to become poor and destitute, went a journey. One day he arrived in a desert, and saw a lion wallowing by the side of a pond, with a fox and a deer standing before him. The Brahmin was confounded, and stood dreading *the consequence*. Suddenly the fox and deer espied the Brahmin; they said to one another, If the lion sees, he will kill this poor helpless fellow;

مصلحت آنست که حکمتي سازيم تا شير اورا نکشد و هيچ چيز انعام

advisable it is that some contrivance we may form that the lion him may uot kill only, but some donation

دهد آهو و روبا شيررا دعا کردن گرفتند که سخاوت تو چنان مشهور

grant. The deer and fox the lion to bless - began saying, The munificence of you so renowned

شده است که امروز برهمني آمده است و اميدوار انعام استاده

is, that to-day a Brahmin is come, and in shope of a gift is standing

شير بر برهمن نظر کرد و اورا نزد خود طلبيد و بسيار مهرباني نمود

the lion at the Brahmin looked and him near him called, and great kindness shewed.

آن مردمان را که پيشتر کشته بود زر و زيورات آنها افتاده بود به

The men who before had been slain, the gold and jewels of them lying about on

برهمن بخشيد و رخصت نمود بخانهٔ خود آمد بعد چند روز

the Brahmin he bestowed and dismissed (him); at his own house he arrived. After-wards some days,

برهمن بطمع زر باز پيش شير مذکور رفت آن روز گرگ و سگان

the Brahmin thirsting for gold again to the lion aforesaid went. That day a wolf and some dogs

پيش شير حاضر بودند چون برهمن را ديدند عرض کردند که اين

on the lion attending were; when the Brahmin they saw they said, This

ایک ایسي مصلحت کیجیي' کہ وہ جس کے باعث اس کو نہ ماری
بلکہ انعام دی . یہہ بات تھراکر شیر کو دعاییں دیکر کہنے لگیں کہ
سخاوت آپ کی یہاں تک مشہور هویئ هي کہ آج ایک برهمن
بھي کچھہ مانگنے آیا هي اور هاتھہ باند هي سامہني کھڑا هي . شیر
نے سر اٹھا کر دیکھا اور خوش هوکر اس برهمن کو آگی بلایا اور نہایت
رحم کھایا . غرض زر و زیور ان لوگوں کا کہ جنہیں مارا تھا . سب
کا سب اس برهمن کو بخشا اور مہرباني سے رخصت کیا تب وہ
برهمن بہت سامال لیکر اپني گھر گیا اور مزي سے گذران کرنے
لگا . بعد ایک مدت کي پھیر جو لالچ هوا تو وہ برهمن اجل گرفتہ اسے
شیر کے پاس گیا اس وقت اسکي سامہني بھیڑیي اور کتي کھڑی تھی .
اس برهمن کو دیکھتے هي خوش هوئ اور شیر سے کہنے لگے کہ یہہ

it is advisable that we fall on some contrivance that the lion may not only spare his life, but grant him some donation. The deer and fox began blessing the lion; Your munificence is so renowned, that a Brahmin is come to day, and is in hopes of a gift. The lion looked at the Brahmin, told him to approach, and shewed him great kindness. He saw, lying about, the gold and jewels of men who had been slain some time before; these he bestowed on the Brahmin, and then gave him leave to depart. The Brahmin arrived at his own house. Some days afterwards, the Brahmin, thirsting for gold, went again to this lion. That day a wolf and some dogs were attending on the lion; when these saw the Brahmin, they said, This

آدم نهایت گستاخ است که بي طلب نزد شما آمده است شیر

man very presump-tuous is uninvited before you to appear The lion

غصه شد و بر جست و برهمن را پاره پاره کرد

enraged was and sprang up and the Brahmin in pieces tore.

طوطي چون این حکایت تمام کرد خجسته را گفت که برهمن اگر

The parrot when this story had con-cluded, to Kho-jisteh he said, The Brahmin if

طمع نکردی کشته نشدي و هر که طمع میکند در بلاي ها مي افتاد

avaricious had not been, killed he would not have been; and whosoever covetous is, into calamities falls.

حالا یک پاس شب باقي است اي خجسته جلد برو و با معشوق

Still one watch of the night remaining is; O Khojisteh quickly go and with your lover

ملاقات کرده بیا خجسته برخاست و عزم رفتن کرد همان دم خروس

having met, return. Khojisteh stood up with intention to go; at that instant the cock

آواز کرد و صبح ظاهر شد رفتن او موقوف گشت

crowed and the dawn appearing her depar-ture was de-layed

آدمي کیسا شوخ هي اور کتنا ڈھیتھہ کہ بي آپ کی طلب کیے
روبرو چلا آتا هي اور خطر اپني جان کا نہین کرتا . اِس بات کي
سنتی هي شیر آگ هوگیا اور اپني جگہہ سے اُچھل کر ایک هي
طپانچي سے اُس برهمن کا کام تمام کیا
توتي نی یہہ نقل تمام کرکي کہا کہ خجستہ اگر وہ برهمن لالچ نہ
کرتا تو جان سے نہ مارا جاتا . یقین هي جو لالچ کریگا سو بلا میں
پڑیگا . خیر اب پہر رات باقي هي جلد جا اور اپنی معشوق سے
مل آ اور اِتني رات عیش و عشرت میں بسر کر . خجستہ نی
یہہ سنتي هي چاها کہ جاوي اور اُسي اپني گلي لگاوي اِتني میں
پو پهتي اور صبح هوئي مرغ نے بانگ دی جانا اُس کا اُس روز بهي
موقوف هوا تب یہہ بیت پڑهي اور رونی لگي .
وصل کي شب کو کیون گنواتي هي . اي سحر کس لیي تو آتي هي .

man is exceedingly presumptuous to appear before you uninvited. The lion was enraged, sprang up, and tore the Brahmin in pieces."

The parrot having concluded the story, said to Khojisteh, "If the Brahmin had not been avaricious, he would not have lost his life; whosoever is covetous, falls into calamities. One watch of the night is still remaining, go quickly, meet your lover and return."

Khojisteh stood up with intention to go; at that instant the cock crowed, and the dawn appearing, her departure was delayed.

PERSIAN.		HINDOOSTANEE.
نقل ۲	**STORY II.**	۲ نقل
شخصي نزد طبيب رفت	A person went to a physician,	ایک شخص طبیب کے پاس گیا
و گفت شکم من درد میکند	and, complaining of a pain in his bowels,	کہا حکیم جي میری پیٹ میں درد هي
دوا کن	asked for some medicine	دوا کیجیي
طبیب پرسید امروز چه خوردهٔ	The physician asked, what he had eaten that day;	اسنے پوچھا کہو آج تم نے کیا غذا کھای تھی
گفت نان سوخته	and he answered, Burnt bread.	کہا اور تو کچھه نہیں مگر ایک جلي روٹي
طبیب دوا در چشم او کردن خواست	The doctor wanted to apply some medicine to the man's eyes,	تب وہ اسکے آنکھوں میں دواي لگانے لگا
آن شخص گفت	when he said,	مریض بولا
اي طبیب درد شکم را با چشم چه نسبت	O Doctor ! what connection is there between the belly-ach and the eyes?	بھلا پیٹ کي درد کو آنکھوں سے کیا نسبت
حکیم گفت اول دواي چشم مي باید کرد	The doctor answered, You first require medicine for your eyes;	طبیب نے کہا پہلی آنکھوں کے دوا ضرور هي

PERSIAN.		HINDOOSTANEE.
زيرا كه اگرچشمت درست بودي	because, if they had seen perfectly,	كيونكه جو آنكهيں اچهيں هوتين
نان سوخته نمي خوردي	you would not have eaten burnt bread.	توتم جلي هوئي روٹي هرگز نه كهاتے
نقل ٣	STORY III.	٣ نقل
شخصي نوكر خود را گفت	A person said to his servant,	ايک نے اپنے نوكر كو كها
كه علي الصباح اگر دو زاغ را يک جا نشسته بيني	If you see two crows together early in the morning,	نور كے تڑكے دو كوى ايک جگهه جهاں بيٹهے
	apprize me of it,	ديكهه
مرا خبر كن		تو مجهه خبر كر
كه آنها را خواهم ديد	that I may also behold them	ميں اُن كو ديكهونگا
و شكون نيك خواهم يافت	as it will be a good omen,	شكون نيک هي
تمام روز مرا بخوشي خواهد گذشت	whereby I shall pass the whole day pleasantly.	سارا دن بخوشي گذريگا
القصه نوكراو دو زاغ را يكجا ديد . صاحب خود را خبر داد	In short, the servant saw two crows in one place; he informed his master;	اس كے چاكر نے دو كوى ايک ساتهه بيٹهے جو ديكهے جا خبر كے
صاحب او چون بيرون آمد	but when the latter came,	وه جو آكر

PERSIAN.		HINDOOSTANEE.
یک زاغ را دیده	he saw only one,	دیکھے تو ایک کوا بیتھا هي
دیگر زاغ پریده بود	the other having flown away.	دوسرا اڑگیا
بسیار بر نوکر غصه شد	He was very angry,	دیکھه کے بہت برهم درهم هوکر
و تازیانه زدن گرفت	and began to horse-whip the servant;	نوکر کو کوڑی مارنے لگا
همان وقت دوستي براي او طعام فرستاد	at which time a friend sent him some victuals.	اسي وقت اسکے کسے دوست نے کھانا اسکے ليي بهجوایا
نوکر عرض کرد که	The servant said,	نوکرنے عرض کے
اي خداوند یک زاغ را دیدي	O my lord! you saw only one crow,	که خداوند نے ایک کاگ دیکھه کر
طعام یافتي	and have obtained victuals;	کھانے کا خوان پایا
اگر دو زاغ را میدیدي	had you seen two,	جو دو کوے دیکھتے
مي یافتي آنچه من یافتم	you would have met with my fare.	تو یهه پاتي جو میں نہ پایا

STORY IV.

نقل ۴	STORY IV.	۴ نقل
روزي پادشاهي ظالم تنها از شهر بیرون رفت	One day a tyrannic king having gone out of the city unattended,	ایک دن کوئي بادشاه ظالم تنها شهر سے باهر گیا

PERSIAN.		HINDOOSTANEE.
شخصي را زير درختي نشسته ديد	saw a person sitting under a tree,	كسي آدمي كو نيچے درخت كي بيٹها ديكها
پرسيد كه پادشاه اين ملك چگونه است ظالم يا عادل	of whom he enquired, What is the character of the king of this country? is he oppressive, or just?	پوچها كه بادشاه اس ملك كا ظالم هي كه عادل
گفت بسيار ظالم است	He answered, a great tyrant.	اس نے كها سخت ظالم
پادشاه گفت مرا مي شناسي	The king said, Do you know me?	بادشاه نے فرمايا تو مجهه پهچانتا هي
گفت نه	He answered, No.	كها نهين
پادشاه گفت منم سلطان اين ملك	The king rejoined, I am the monarch of this place.	بولا مين اس ملك كا بادشاه هون
آن مرد ترسيد و پرسيد مرا ميداني	The man was terrified, and asked, Do you know who I am?	وه ڈرا اور كها مجهے جانتے هو
پادشاه گفت نه	The king said, he did not.	كها نهين
گفت پسر فلان سوداگرام	He rejoined, I am the son of such a merchant;	كها مين فلانے سوداگر كا بيتا هون
هر ماه سه روز ديوانه ميشوم	three days in every month I lose my senses,	تين دن هر مهينے مين ديوانه هو جاتا هون
امروز يكي از آن سه روز است	and this is one of those three days.	سو آج كا دن بهي انهين تين مين سے هي

PERSIAN.		HINDOOSTANEE.
پادشاه خندید واورا هیچ نگفت	The king laughed, and ended the conversation.	بادشاه نے هنس دیا اور کچهه نه کہا
نقل ٥	STORY V.	٥ نقل
نابینایي در شب تار	A blind man in a dark night,	اندهیری رات میں ایک اندها
چراغ در دست و سبو بر سر گرفته	having taken a lamp in his hand, and an earthen jar on his head,	هاتهه میں چراغ اور سر پر گهڑا لیۓ
در بازار میرفت	was going into the market-place.	بازار میں چلا جاتا تها
شخصي ازوي پرسید	Somebody said to him,	ایک شخص نے اس سے پوچها
که اي حمق روز و شب درچشم تو یکسان است	You blockhead, day and night are the same in your eyes;	سن تو اي بیوقوف تیری نزدیک رات دن برابر هي
از چراغ ترا فایدۂ چیست	of what use can a lamp be to you?	تجهی دیۓ سے کیا فایدۂ
نابینا خندید و گفت این چراغ براي من نیست بلکه براي تست	The blind man laughing, replied, this lamp is not intended for my own, but for your use,	بولا یهه دیا میری واسطی نهیں بلکه تمهاری لیۓ هي
تا در شب تار سبوي مرا نشکني	in order that in this dark night, you may not break my jar.	کیونکه اندهیری رات میں کهیں میری گهڑی کو نه توڑ ڈالو

PERSIAN.		HINDOOSTANEE.
نقل ٦	## STORY VI.	٦ نقل
دزدی در مقام شخصي براي دزديدن اسپ رفت	One day a thief went to the dwelling of a certain person in order to steal a horse.	ايک چور کسے کے يہاں گھوڑا چرانے گيا تھا
اتفاقا گرفتار شد	He happened to be seized;	قضا کار وه پکڑا گيا
صاحب اسپ دزد را گفت	and the owner of the horse told him,	گھوڑی والي نے اسے کہا
اگر حکمت دزدي اسپ مرا بنمايي	that if he would show him how he contrived to steal a horse,	جو تين مجھی گھوڑا چرانا سکھاوے
ترا ازاد بکنم	he should be released.	تو مين تجھی چھوڑ دون
دزد قبول کرد و نزد اسپ رفت و رسن پاي او کشاد	He consented, and approached the horse and cast off the heel-ropes,	چور نے مانا گھوڑي کا پابند جاکر کھولا
بعد از آن لگام داد پس بر اسپ سوار شد	he then put the bridle in his mouth, after which he mounted,	لگام ديکر سوار هوا
و تيز راند و گفت	and putting the horse in full speed, cried out,	اور چڑھتی هي کہا
ببين اين طور دزدي ميکنند	"Behold! this is the way that I steal;"	ديکھو اس طرح چراتے هين يہه کہتے هي گھوڑا دوڑايا بھتيرا
مردمان هر چند که تعاقب او کردند نيافتند	and all that the people could do in pursuit of him they could not come up with him.	سواروں نے پيچھا اس کا کيا پر اسے نه پايا

PERSIAN.		HINDOOSTANEE.
نقل ۷	STORY VII.	نقل ۷
روزي پادشاهي مع شاهزاده	One day a king and his son	کسے دن بادشاه اور شہزادہ رمنے میں دونو
بشکار رفت	went a hunting.	شکار کھیلنے کو گیي
چون هوا گرم شد	The weather being hot,	گرمي جو بہت ہوی
پادشاه و شاهزاده لبادهٔ خودرا بردوش مسخرهٔ نهادند	they put their fur cloaks on the back of a jester.	اپنا اور شہزادی کا دو شالا اتار کر ایک مسخری کي حوالي کیا اسنے کاندھے پر دھر لیا
پادشاه تبسم کرد وگفت	The king smiled and said to the buffoon,	تب اس سے ہنسکر کہا که ایک گدھے کا بوجھه
اي مسخره بر تو بار یک خر است	You have the load of an ass upon you.	تو تجھه پر ہوا ہوگا
گفت بلکه بار دو خر	He answered, yes, or rather the burden of two asses.	اس نے جواب دیا خداوند ایک کا نہیں بلکه دو کا

Preface to the Gulistan of MUSLEH-UD-DEEN SHEIKH SAADI of Shiraz.

بسم الله الرّحمن الرّحيم

In the name of God the Clement, the Merciful.

PERSIAN.		HINDOOSTANEE.
منّت خدايرا عزّ و جلّ	Praise to the God of majesty and glory,	شكر و احسان هي خدا كا كه غالب هي سب پر اور بزرگ هي سب سي
كه طاعتش موجب قربتست	whose service is the means of approach!	طاعت اسكي سبب هي قرب كا
و بشكر اندرش مزيد نعمت	and to offer him grateful acknowledgements, insures an increase of bounty.	اور شكر اسكا زياده كرني والا هي نعمت كا
هر نفسي كه فرو مي رود	Every breath when inhaled,	جو دم كه نيچي حلق كي جاتا هي
ممدّ حيات است	sustaineth life;	مدد گار حيات كا هي
و چون بر مي آيد	and when respired,	اور جو اوپر آتا هي
مفرّح ذات	it exhilarates the body:	فرح بخش ذات كا
پس در هر نفسي	consequently every breathing	پس هر ايك سانس مين
دو نعمت موجود است	includes two benefits,	دو نعمتين موجود هين

PERSIAN.		HINDOOSTANEE.
و بر هر نعمتي شكري واجب	each of which demands a distinct acknowledgement.	اور هر ايك نعمت پر ايك شكر واجب
بيت	*A Distich.*	بيت
از دست و زبان كه بر آيد * كز عهدهٔ شكرش بدر آيد *	What hand or tongue can fulfil his praise?	عبد كي دست و زبان هين چيز كيا * شكر سي اسكي جو هو عهده برا *
قوله تعالي اعملوا آل داوٗد شكراً	Sing praises, ye posterity of David, saith the Lord,	چنانچه خداي تعالي كهتا هي عمل شايسته كرو اي آل داوٗد ايسي نعمتون كي شكر مين
و قليل من عبادي الشكور	for few of my servants are grateful.	اور ميري بندي شكر گذار تهوڙي هين
قطعه	*A Strophe.*	قطعه
بنده همان به كه ز تقصير خويش * عذر بدرگاهٔ خدا آورد * ورنه سزاوار خداونديش * كس نتواند كه بجا آورد *	It is best for the servant to confess his weakness, and implore forgiveness at the court of heaven, since no one is able to fulfil his duty towards God.	خوب هي بنده وهي جو عجز سي * در په صاحب كي كري عذر خطا * ورنه لايق صاحبي كي اسكي يهان * كس سي هو سكتا هي جو لاوي بجا *

PERSIAN.		HINDOOSTANEE.
با را ن رحمت بي حسابش همه را فرا رسيده	The rain of his infinite mercy refreshes all places;	اسكي رحمت بـــي حساب كا ميهه سبهونپر برسا هي
و خوان الوان نعمت بيد ريغش	and the table of his bounty	اور اسكي نعمت بي دريغ كا دستر خوان
همه جا كشيده	is spread far and near.	سب جگهه بچها هي
وپردهٔ ناموس بندگان بگناهٔ فاحش ندرد	Amidst the enormous sins of his servants, he rendeth not the veil of their reputation;	بندونكي ناموس كا پرده بهٔ سبب گناهٔ فاحش كي نهين پهاڑتا
ووظيفهٔ روزي خواران بخطاي منكر نبرد	and during the commission of atrocious offences, ceaseth not to bestow their daily bread.	اور روزينه كسيكي روزيكا خطائي زشت كي باعث بند نهين كرتا
قطعه	*A Strophe.*	قطعه
اي كريمي كه از خزانهٔ غيب * گبر و ترسا وظيفه خورداري * دوستان را كجا كني محروم * تو كه با دشمنان نظر داري *	O merciful God, who out of thine hidden treasures, affordest daily sustenance to the Guebre and the infidel, how canst thou exclude thy friends; thou who deignest thus favourably to regard thine enemies!	تيري خزانهٔ غيبي سي اي خداي كريم * مدام پاتي هين روزينه گبر اور ترسا * محال هي كه تيري دوست تجهي هون محروم * كه اپني دشمنون كو نعمتين تو هي ديتا *

PERSIAN.		HINDOOSTANEE.
فرّاش باد صبا را گفت	He commandeth his chamberlain, the zephyr,	باد صبا کي فرّاش کو ارشاد کیا
تا فرش زمردین بکسترد	to spread the emerald carpet,	که فرش زمرّدي بچهاوي
و دایهٔ ابر بهاري را فرمود	and ordereth the vernal clouds	اور دایهٔ ابر بهارکو فرمایا
تا بنات نبات را در مهد زمین به پرورد	to foster the infant plants in the cradle of the earth.	که هر روئیدگي کو درختان شیرخوارکي مانند زمین کي پالني مین پالي
و درختان را بخلعت نوروزي قباي سبزورق دربرگرفته	He clotheth the bodies of the trees with verdant foliage, the festal garments of spring;	درختونکیتین نوروزکو خلعت سبز پتونکا پنهایا
واطفال شاخرا بقدوم موسم بهاري کلاهٔ شکوفه برسر نهاده	and, in celebration of the return of that season, crowneth the youthful branches with garlands of blossoms.	اور موسم بهار کي آني سي شگوفي کا تاج اطفال شاخ کي سرپر رکّها
وعصارهٔ تاکي بقدرتش شهد فایق گشته	By his power the juice of the vine is converted into delicious honey;	شیره انگور کا اسکي قدرت سي شهد خالص هوا
وتخم خرما بتربیّتش نخل باسق بلند شده	and the kernel of the date by his instruction, becometh a lofty palm tree.	اور تخم خرما اسّکي پرورش سي نخل بلند بالا

PERSIAN.

قطعه

ابر و باد و مه و خورشيد و فلك در كارند * تا تو ناني بكف آري و بغفلت نخوري * همه از بهر تو سرگشته و فرمان بردار * شرط انصاف نباشد كه تو فرمان نبري *

A Strophe.

Clouds and wind, the moon, the sun, and the sky, are all busied that thou, O man, mayest obtain thy bread, and eat it not in neglect. For thy sake all these revolve and are obedient; it is not therefore consistent with the rules of justice that thou only shouldst not obey.

HINDOOSTANEE.

قطعه

ابر و باد و فلك و شمس و قمر كام مين هين * كه تو روتي كو جو پيدا كري غفلت سي نه كهائي * هينگي سرگشته و محكوم سبهي تيري ليي * منصفي يهه نهين جو حكم سي تو يون پهر جاي *

در خبراست از سرور كائنات و مفخر موجودات

There is a tradition of the chief of created beings, the most noble of existences,

سردار كائنات كا فخر موجودات كا

رحمت عالميان و صفوت آدميان وتتمهٔ دور زمان محمّد مصطفي عليه الصّلوة والسّلام

the mercy of the universe, the purest of mankind, and completion of the revolution of ages, Mohammed Mustafa, (upon whom be blessing and peace!)

باعث رحمت عالميونكا برگزيده آدميون كا تتمّه زمانيكا

شعر

شفيع مطاع نبي كريم * قسيم جسيم بسيم و نسيم *

Verse.

The intercessor, the obeyed, the gracious prophet, the bountiful, the majestic, the affable, the sealed.

شعر

شفيع و قاسم نارو جنان نبيّ كريم * شكيل و سرور و خنده دهان خليق و جسيم *

PERSIAN.		HINDOOSTANEE.
چه غم دیوار امت را که باشد چون تو پشتیبان * چه باک از موج بحر آن را که باشد نوح کشتیبان *	Why should the wall of the faithful suffer anxiety which has such a supporter? Why should he dread the waves of the sea who has Noah for his pilot?	گري ديوار امت کب سهارا اسکو هي تيرا * ڈري وه موج سي کيون نوح هووي نا خدا جسکا *
بلغ العلي بکماله * کشف الدجي بجماله * حسنت جميع خصاله * صلواة عليه و آله *	His perfections procured him exaltation, his comeliness dispelled the darkness; liberal are all his endowments, blessing be on him and on his race.	رتبهٔ عالي کيتين پهنچا هي اس شه کا کمال * ظلمتين کرتا هي روشن اسکا نوراني جمال * نيک هينگي سربسر اس پاك طينت کي خصال * لايق صلواة وه هيگا فقط اور اسکي آل *
هرگاه که يکي از بندگان گنه کار پريشان روزگار دست انابت بامید اجابت بدرگاه حق جل بردارد	The tradition is this; That when a sinful servant, conscious of his guiltiness, lifteth up the hands of repentance, in hopes of obtaining pardon at the court of the just, the glorious, and sublime Being.	يونکهتا هي که جو کويي بندهٔ گنه گار پريشان روزگار درگاه مين خداي بزرگ و برترکي هاتهه کارهاي بد سي کهينچ کر اجابت کي اميد پر پهيلاوي
ايزد تعالي در وي نظر نکند	the Almighty regardeth him not;	حق تعالي اسپر نظر لطف کي نکري

PERSIAN.		HINDOOSTANEE.
بازش بخواند باز اعراض کند	again he supplicates, and is again disregarded:	پهر اسکي جناب مين اگرزاري کري تب بهي روبي رحمت پهيرلي
بازش بتضرع و زاري بخواند	once more he prayeth with humility and sorrow,	اسپر بهي وه تضرّع سي هاتهه نه اتهايي اور پهر اسطرح عاجزسي گڑگڑاي
حق سبحانه تعالي گويد يا ملايکتي بقد استحييت من عبدي	and then the just God saith, "O my angels, of a truth I am ashamed on behalf of my servant,	تب خدا اي کريم کهي اي فرشتو حيا کي مين ني اپني بندي سي
و ليس له رب غيري	who hath no other Providence than myself,	که نهين هي اسکا ربّ کويي اورسواي ميري
فقد غفرت له	and therefore verily do I pardon him.	پس بخشامين ني اسکو دعا اسکي قبول کي
دعوتش را اجابت کردم و حاجتش را آوردم	I have heard his prayer, and have granted his petition;	اورحاجت اسکي برلايا
که ازبسياري دعا وزاري بنده شرم هميدارم	because I am ashamed of the excessive supplication and sorrow of my servant."	که اپني بندي کي کثرة دعا سي اورزاري سي شرماتا هون
بيت	*A Distich.*	بيت
کرم بين ولطف خداوند گار * گنه بنده کرده است و او شرمسار *	Behold the mercy and kindness of God, he is himself ashamed that his servant hath sinned!	ديکهه توکيا کچهه هي لطف کردگار * عبد هين عاصي وه هيگا شرمسار *

PERSIAN.		HINDOOSTANEE.
عاكفان كعبهٔ جلالش	Those who constantly reside at the temple of his glory,	معتكف اسكي كعبهٔ جلال كي
بتقصير عبادت معترف اند	confess the insufficiency of their worship,	اپني عبادت كي قصور پر مقر هين كه
كه ما عبدناك حق عبادتك	saying, "We have not worshipped thee in the manner that thou oughtest to be served."	عبادت نهين لي همني تيري جو حق عبادتكا هي
و واصفان حليهٔ جمالش بتحير منسوب	And they who describe the form of his beauty, are rapt in amazement, declaring,	اور وصف كرني والي اسكي جمال كي حيران هوكر كهتي هين
كه ما عرفناك حق معرفتك	"We have not known thee as thou oughtest to be known."	كه نهين پهچانا همني حق تيري معرفت كا
قطعه	*A Strophe.*	قطعه
گر كسي وصف او ز من پرسد * بي دل از بي نشان چه گويد باز * عاشقان كشتگان معشوقند * بر نيايد ز كشتگان اواز	If any one should require me to describe him, how shall the disheartened describe that which hath no form? The lovers are slain by the beloved, and no voice proceedeth from the dead.	جو كوئي مجسي پوچهي اسكا وصف * بي نشان كا پتا بتاؤن كيا * هينگي عشّاق كشتهٔ معشوق * كب نكلتي هي كشتگان كي صدا
حكايت	*A Fable.*	حكايت
يكي از صاحبدلان سر بجيب مراقبه فرو برده بود	A devout man in deep contemplation, with his head reclined on the bosom of meditation,	ايک صاحب دل مراقبي مين گيا تها

PERSIAN.		HINDOOSTANEE.
و در بحر مکاشفه مستغرق شده	was immersed in the ocean of vision,	اور کشف کے دریا میں ڈوبا تھا
آنگاه که از آن حالت باز آمد	When he recovered from that state,	جسوقت که اس حالت سے نکلا
یکي از اصحاب بطریق انبساط اورا گفت	one of his companions by way of pleasantry said,	ایك اسکے هم صحبت نے گستاخي سے کہا
از آن بوستان که توبودي مارا چه تحفۀ کرامت آوردي	"What miraculous present have you brought us from this garden, which you have been visiting?"	جس باغمین که تو تها وهانسے همارے واسطے کیا تحفه لایا
گفت بخاطر داشتم	He answered "It was my intention,	کہا اسنے اراده تها
که چون بدرخت گل برسم	that when I reached the rose bush,	که جب پهولونکے درخت تک پہنچونگا
دامني پر کنم هدیۀ اصحاب را برم	I would fill my lap with flowers, for presents to my friends;	یارونکے واسطے دامن بهرلونگا
چون برسیدم بوي گلم چنان مست کرد	but when I came to the spot, the odour so overpowered my senses,	جب که پہنچا گل کي پاس نے ایسا مست کیا
که دامنم از دست برفت	that my skirt dropt out of my hands."	که دامن میری هاتهه سے چهٹ گیا

PERSIAN.

ابيات

گفتم كه گلي بچينم از باغ * گل ديدم و مست گشتم از بوي * اي مرغ سحر عشق ز پروانه بياموز * كان سوخته را جان شد و آواز نيامد *

اين مدعيان در طلبش بيخبرانند * كانراكه خبر شد خبرش باز نيامد *

اي برتر از خيال و قياس و گمان و وهم * وز هرچه گفته اند شنيديم و خوانده ايم *

مجلس تمام گشت بپايان رسيد عمر * ما همچنان در اوّل وصف تو مانده ايم *

Verses.

I said, I will pluck a rose from the garden: I saw a rose, and was overcome with its fragrance. O bird of the desert learn thou love of the moth, who being burnt, expireth without a sigh.

They who pretend to be informed, are ignorant, for they who have known him, have not yet recovered their senses. O, thou art beyond the reach of imagination, conjecture, or thought; surpassing all that has been related, and excelling every thing that I have heard or read.

The banquet is concluded, and the period of life is arrived. I continue describing thee the same as at the commencement.

HINDOOSTANEE.

ابيات

مين چاها كه باغ سے چنون پهول * گل ديكهه كے بو سے هو گيا مست * تو سيكهه چلن عشق كے پروانے سے بلبل * وه چلكے هوا راكهه پهر آواز نه آيي *

يهه مدعي آگاه نهين عشق سے مطلق * واقف جو هويي انكي خبر پهير نه پايي * اي وهم اور قياس سے باهر گمانسے دور * بلكه جو كچهه كه همنے سنا اورهي پڑها *

مجلس تمام هوگيي اور عمر پر تيري * پهلے هي وصف مين مين رها جسطرح سے تها *

PERSIAN.	HINDOOSTANEE.

اوصاف بادشاه اسلام کہ همیشه رکهےالله ملک اسکا

ذکر جمیل سعدي که در افواه عوام
افتاده وصیت سخنش که در بسیط
زمین رفته و قصب الجیب حدیثش
که همچون نیشکر میخورند و رقعهٔ
منشاتش که چون کاغذ زر میبرند
بر کمال فضل و بلاغت او حمل نتوان
کرد بلکه خداوند جهان وقطب دایرهٔ
زمان و قایم مقام سلیمان و ناصر
اهل ایمان اتابك اعظم شهنشاه معظم
مظفر الدنیا و الدین ابوبکر بن سعد
بن زنگي ظل اللهتعالي في ارضه رب
الارض ارض عنه

سعدیکي خوبیونکا چرچا که عوام
میں اسقدر پهیلا هي اور آوازه اسکے
کلام کا اکثر ملکوں میں پهنچا هي.
شیریني اسکے سخن کي مثل شکر
کے کهاتےهیں اور پرزی اسکي نظم و
نثر کے هنڈي کے کاغذ کي مانند
لیجاتے هیں. سبب اسکا فضل وکمال
اسکا نهیں بلکه خداوند جهان
قطب دایرهٔ زمان جا نشین سلیمان
مددگار اهل ایمان شاهنشاه عظیم
الشان اتابك اعظم یعنے اتالیق بزرگتر
مظفر الدین ابوبکر بن سعد زنگي نے
سایه خداي بزرگ کا رهي

The virtues of the Monarch of Islamism, may God perpetuate his reign.

The favourable mention of Saadi which has fallen from the mouths of people in general, and the fame of his sayings that has spread over the whole surface of the globe, so that the words of his friendly pen are eaten like sugar; and the value given to his scraps of writings, insomuch that they pass current like bills of exchange: all this cannot be ascribed to the perfection of his own merit and eloquence, but is owing to the monarch of the earth, who is the axis of the revolution of time,* the representative of Solomon, the defender of the faithful, the mighty king of kings, the illustrious Atabuk Mozafferuddeen Aboobeker, the son of Saad, the son of Zengi, the shadow of God on earth; approve him, O Lord, and grant his desires!

PERSIAN.	HINDOOSTANEE.
بعين عنايت نظر كرده و تحسين بليغ فرموده لاجرم كافهٔ انام از خواص و عوام بمحبت او گراينده اند كه الناس علي دين ملوكهم	ملكوں پر اسكے اي پروردگار خوش ره اتنے اور خوش ركهه آسكو چشم عنايت سے اسپر نظر كي هي اور صدق ارادت سے تحسين و آفرين بهت سے فرمايي هي اسواسطے ناچار تمام خلق كو اسكي محبت پر رغبت هويي كه الناس علي دين ملوكهم يعني آدمي اپنے پادشاهونكے رويے اور طريقے پر چلتے هيں
شعر	شعر
زانگه كه ترا بر من مسكين نظر است آثارم از آفتاب مشهورتر است گر خود همه عيبها بدين بنده در است هر عيب كه سلطان بپسندد هنر است	جب سے كه مجهه گدا پر شاها تيري نظر هي. شهره جهان ميں ميرا خور سے زياده تر هي. هيں عيب جتنے جگميں وه مجهه ميں هيں سراسر. ليكن جو عيب شهكو بهاوے وهي هنر هي.

He regarded me with the eye of kindness, loaded me with commendation, and shewed a sincere attachment; and therefore, for his sake, persons of all descriptions have taken a fancy to me; for mankind readily adopt the sentiments of their king.

Verses.

From the time that you have looked kindly on my humble state, my merits are more manifest than the sun.

If your servant was made up of defects, every fault that the sultan might commend, would be construed into an excellence.

HINDOOSTANEE

FAMILIAR PHRASES

AND

DIALOGUES.

FAMILIAR PHRASES.

سلام عليكم or صاحب سلام	Peace be with you Sir.
عليكم السلام	To you be peace.
كيسا هي	How do you do?
تمهارا عمر كيا	How old are you?
جوان تم هي	You are a young man.
همسے تم اور بڑا هي	You are older than I.
تمهارا طبيعت خير هي	Do you enjoy good health?
تم كبهي كبهي بي آرام هي	Are you ever ill?
تمهارا باپ جيتا هي	Is your father living?
تمهارا ما مرگيا	Is your mother dead?
تم شادي كيا	Are you married?
كچھ لڑكا لڑكي هين	Have you any children?
كتنا گهڑي هي	What o'clock is it?

چہار گھڑي ھي	It is four g,hurries (about an hour and half after sun-rise).
دو پہر ھي	It is two pahars. (noon)
شام ھوا	It is sun-set.
برسات کا آیام ھي	It is the rainy season.
گرمي کا آیام ھي	It is the hot season.
سردي کا آیام ھي	It is cold
اولا ھي	It hails.
بہوکہا ھمکو لگتا ھي	I am hungry
ھم کہانا مانگتا	I want something to eat
ھم کیا کہاونگا	What shall I eat?
پیاسا ھمکو لگتا	I am thirsty
ھم کیا پیونگا	What shall I drink?
پینا کو دی	Give me something to drink
بس ھي	It is enough
اور ھم نہیں مانگتا	I want no more

کیا خبر هي	What news?
اچها خبر هي	Is there any good news?
لشکرسے خبر هي،	There is news from the army
دشمن بهاگا هي	The enemy has fled
یهه سچ هي	Is this true?
شهر کا بات کیا	What is the town's chat?
جهاز کا خبر کیا	What is the ship news?
وه کیا هي	What is that?
کچهه هي نهین	It is nothing
چهوتا کام هي	It is of little consequence
کون شهوره کرتا	What noise is that?
تم کیا کهتا	What do you say?
کسواسطے ایسا کهتا	Why does he say so?
تم همکو بوجهتا	Do you understand me?
هم تم کو بوجهتا نهین	I do not understand you
کیا کهتا بول	Tell (me) what he says

شور سے بول Speak loud

تم کو مین سننا سکتا نہین I cannot hear you

ایسا شورش مت کر Do not make such a noise

تم بہت دھیما بولتا You speak very low

دو ایک کہتا مت بول Do not speak both together

ایک پہلا مین سنونگا I will first hear one

عربي تم کہتا سکتا Can you speak arabic?

هم تمکو بوجھه سکتے نہین I cannot understand you

پهیر اوسکو بول Repeat what you said

آهسته بول Speak deliberately

بهت جلدي تم بولتا You speak too fast

پاجي هندوستاني بول Speak low hindoostanee

نرم هندوستاني بول Speak easy hindoostanee

تم گونجتا You stammer

چپ کر Be silent

همارا سر کو تم پهاڑتا You distract me

اسکا حقیقت کو مین سنونگا	I will hear his tale
اورهم ابهي سننا سکتا نہین	I cannot hear any more now
دوسرا هم کل سنینگي	I will hear the rest tomorrow
کہان سے آیا	Whence came you?
کدهر جاتا	Whither are you going?
ادهر آو	Come here
اودهر جاؤ	Go thither
جلدي کر	Make haste
آهسته جاؤ	Take time
بازار کو جاؤ	Go to market
جلدي پهير آو	Return quickly
فلان صاحب کے پاس جاؤ	Go to Mr. —'s
دهینا — باءیان جاؤ	Go to the right-- to the left
برسات آتا	It is going to rain
بڑا جهڑي هي	It rains in torrents
بهت گرم هي	It is very hot

بہت جاڑا هي	It is very cold
بڑا کوهاسا هي	There is a dense fog
بڑا اوس هي	There is a heavy dew
بادل سب گیا	The clouds have dispersed
دهوپ هي	It is sun-shine
وہ کسکا گھر هي	Whose house is that?
جواب دی	Tell me
جواب کسواسطی دینا نہین	Why do you not answer me?
وہ سچ هي	Is that true?
سچ هي	It is true
جهوٹهہ هي	It is false
هم اعتبار سکتی نہین	I cannot believe it
تم کو کون کہا دیا	Who told you?
اورلک هم پوچهینگی	I will inquire of other people
تم جهوٹهہ کہتا مین البتہ سزا دیونگا	If you tell an untruth I will certainly punish you.

DIALOGUE I.

خرید کرنا اور بیچني کا	*Of buying and selling.*
کیا چیز هي تمهارا دکان مین	What articles have you in your shop?
مهربان کیا آپ مانگتے هو	What do you please to want?
تمهارا پاس کچھ اچها مهین بانات ستهري پٹیاں ٹوپیاں اور موزي هین	Have you any fine woollen cloth handsome ribbons, hats, or stockings?
هاں صاحب هین شهر کا اوپر یه شهر مین اور اچها تم سکتے نهین ملنیکا	Yes sir, I have, as good as any in this town: you cannot find better in the place.
یه سچ هي	Indeed?
هاں صاحب سچ هي	Yes sir, it is true.
دکهلاو همکو ایک تهان اچها بانات کالا رنگ	Shew me a piece of fine black cloth.
یه ایک تهان هي مهین بانات صاحب اور اسکا رنگ مین بوجهتا هون آپ کے پسند مین هووي	Here is an excellent piece, sir, and the colour I think will please you.

کیا مول تم بستے ہو	How do you sell it?
کیا در اسکا گز	What is it a yard?
اسکا ٹھیک درھي آٹھہ روپیه	It is really worth eight rupees.
کیا آٹھہ روپیه ان هویگا نهین صاحب تم بوجهتے هو همکو ایسا امي هین	What! eight rupees? Impossible sir, do you think I am so ignorant?
نهین صاحب معاف کرو همك نے مانگی بسستا بدیسي آدمي کو جیسا یهان کی آدمیون کو	No sir, pardon me: we sell equally cheap to strangers as to our countrymen.
سچ تم بهت اچها کهتے هو بهایي لیکن اسکا ساتهه اور سات روپیه کا مین دیونگے نهین تم کو	Well, you speak very fair my friend, but I will give you for it only seven rupees.
اِسکا مول همارا پاس زیاده هي صاحب	It cost me more, sir.
مانگتے هو تم ساڑهے سات روپیه لیوگے	Will you take seven and a half?
سچ کهتے هین مین دینی سکونگا نهین آٹهه روپیه کے کم لیکن جو تم میري دکان کي خریدار هو مین تمکو چهوڑ دیونگا	To tell you the truth, I ought not to take less than eight rupees; but as you are my customer, I will give it to you.

موٹیہ سنو بھلا آدمي جاؤ یہ صاحب کے ساتھہ انکي حویلي مین	Porter, do you hear my good man? Go with this gentleman to his residence.
صاحب جو تمھاری کچھ اور دوسرا وقت درکار هووي مهرباني کرکے میري دکان مین پھیر آوگے	Sir, should you want any thing at a future time, do me the favour to use my shop.
اچھا هم آوینگے سلام صاهب	Very well, I will, Good by sir.

DIALOGUE II.

پھرنا کا واسطے	*On taking a walk.*
اي واه کیا ستهری وقت هي آج باغچه مین پهیرنا جو آپ کا مزاج هووي بیبي صاحبون چلین هم لک پهیر کرینگے باغچه مین	O what lovely weather it is to day to take a walk in the garden; if it be agreeable to you, ladies, we will walk thither.
ابهي دهوپ کا جبر بڑا هي رهین تیار جب تک ٹھنڈا هووي	The sun is yet too hot, let us wait till (the air) be cooler.
بہت خوب ۞ اب اچھا ٹھنڈا هوي چلی جاوین	Very well. It is now cooler, let us go.

جو تمهاري خوشي مين تيار هون	If you please, I am ready.
اي واه كيا ستهرا باغچه هي اى دكهو صاحب كيا تحفه هي گلاب كا گاچهه اور كيا تحفه هى اسكا پهول	What a delightful garden! Look sir, how beautiful are the rose-bushes; how charming their blossoms.
مهرباني كركے صاحب بنديگا ايک گلدسته ميري واسطي	Do me the favour sir, to gather a nosegay for me.
اسكا بو همكو بهت اچها لگتا	Its odour is very agreeable
تم اسكو پاوگي اي ليو بيبي صاحب	You shall have it, here it is madam.
بهت سلام صاحب	I thank you sir.
اي اور هي تمهارى واسطى هماري دلربي چهوكري ليو اسكو	Here is another for you my charming girl; accept it.
بهت بهت سلام همهارا ديال	I am much obliged to you sir.
كيا موجه كا جگهه يه هي	What a pleasant spot this is.
كيا تحفه يى گل آبيان هين	What beautiful roses these are.

هم دكهتي ايك رنڈي سكتي خوشي هووي اور ايك مرد سكيگا تماشا كريگا	I perceive a woman might be pleasing, and a man entertaining.
تهوڑا آرام كركے هم لگ خوش هوكے گهر مين جاينگے	When we have rested a little, we shall have the pleasure of returning home.
ابهي ساعت هي جاينگے چلے جاوين هم لگ	It is now time to go, let us depart.

DIALOGUE III.

راه سے طلب كرنا	*On inquiring the road.*
بهابي	My friend?
كيا هي صاحب	Sir.
مهربان يه راه هي كلكته مين جانيكو	Pray does this road lead to Calcutta?
نهين صاحب تم بهولے هو تمهارا راه	No sir, you have come out of the way.

كيا تفاوت	How far?
بلكه كس بهر هوگا	About a mile.
توكوي راه هےگے مين جاونگا	Which way then must I go?
جاوء برابر جبتك تم جنگل كے پاس آوگے تد باياں طرف پهر آوگے	Go straight forward till you come to a wood, then turn to the left.
كچهه دهشت نهين يهان گم نے پهيرنا كو	Is there any danger here abouts?
كچهه نهين صاحب سواي رات كے وقت	None sir, except the darkness of the night.
بهايي مهرباني كركے ديكهاو راه مجهكو تمهارا محنت كا واسطے ميں كچهه ديونگا تمكو	My friend, if you will be so obliging as to shew me the way, I will recompence you for your pains.
اچها صاحب تو چليں هملك	Very well sir, then let us go.
ابهي جو تم يه بات برابر جاوگے تم بهولوگي سكتي نهيں	Now, if you keep this path, you cannot miss the way.
بهت خوب هي يه كچهه لاو جو ميں كهتا تها تمهارا محنت كا واسطي	Very well, here is what I promissed you for your trouble.

بہت سلام صاحب اور مانگتا ہوں تمہارا مسافرت بسلامت هووے	I thank you sir, wishing you a safe journey.
خدا حافظ	Adieu.

DIALOGUE IV.

دو یاروں کے بیچ	*Between two friends.*
کیسا هي صاحب میں بہت خوش ہوں تم کو دیکھنیکو	How do you do sir? I am very glad to see you.
میں اچھا ہون صاحب تمہارا خدمت میں	I am well sir, at your service.
کس طرح تمہارا وقت کاٹاتے ہو یہاں	How do you spend your time here?
جو ابھي میرا پاس کچھہ کام نہیں یہان میں پھرتا ہوں	Having no occupation, I walk about.
تمہارا پاس کس کا ساتھہ جان پہچان هي یہاں	Are you acquainted with any body here?
نہیں صاحب	No sir.
میں کار دیونگا تمکو جان پہچان ہماری دوست کے ساتھہ	I will introduce you to some of my acquaintances.

If it be agreeable to you to do me this kindness, I shall be much obliged to you.	جو تمهارا خوشي هوؤ گرنيكو يه مهرباني ميں بڑا بس هونگا آپ کے پاس
When will you come again to see me?	کب تم آوگے پهير مجهکو ديکهنيکو
I will come again in three days.	ترسوں پهير آونگا
Adieu.	خدا حافظ

DIALOGUE V.

On several subjects.	بهت احوال کا
Groom, have you put the saddle on well?	سايیس تم زين اچها لگايي
Are the girths tight?	فراخي کسا هي
The bridle is not clean.	لگام صاف نهيں
The bit is not bright.	دهانه چمکتا نهيں
The stirrups are dirty	رقاب ميلا هي
The horse falls away;	گهوڑا سوکها جاتا

تم اسکا دانه اچها دیتی نهیں	You do not feed him well.
گهاسیڑا کا تقصیر هي گهاس بس پاینگا نهیں	It is the fault of the grass-cutter, he will not get grass enough.
اُسکا نعل اچها هي	Are his shoes good?
دیکهه ایک ڈهیلا هي	See here is one loose.
آج نعلبند کو لیجاؤ	Take him to-day to the farrier.
اسکا یال سب اُلجن هی	His mane is all tangled.
اسکا دم کنگهي پایا نهیں	His tail is not combed.
تم اچها کهرهرا کرتے نهیں	You do not curry him well.
تم تمهارا کام اور اچها طرح کرینگی نهیں هم تمکو چهوڑ دیینگے	If you do not mind your business better, I shall discharge you.
چمرا کا موزه دی	Give me my boots.
ایڑي کا کانٹا دی	Give me my spurs.
موزه بند کهاں هي	Where are my boot-garters?

چابک دی اور گول توپي	Give me my whip and round hat.
هم گهوڑا پر چڑهینگے	I shall take a ride on horseback.
سایيس کو کهول گهوڑا کو تیار کر	Tell the groom to get the horse ready.
اي سایيس صاحب کا گهوڑا اور سواري کو تیار کر	Groom, you must get (our) master's horse ready, and assemble the equipage.
اگر هم پهر کو پهیر آیي هووینگے نهیں باهر حاضري کهینگے	If I do not return by nine o'clock, I shall breakfast out.
هم گهوڑا کو گهر میں بهیجوا دیینگی اور هم کو پالکي بهیجوا دی بیچ میں تم حاضري کا سرانجام تیار کر	I shall send the horse home, and you must send a palanqeen for me, mean while, prepare breakfast.
حاضري لاو	Bring breakfast.
چا بناو	Make the tea.
یه پاني پهوتا هي	Has this water boiled?
جب سے صاحب گهر میں آیا تب سی پهوتا هي	It has boiled sir, ever since you came home.

مصري دی	Give me some sugar candy.
اور دوده لاو	Bring some more milk.
يه روتي بس پكا نهيں	This bread is not baked enough.
صاحب ميں نانبايي كو پهلا كهتا تها	Sir I told the baker of it before.
پهير كهو	Tell him again.
صاحب وه بهاگا هي	He has absconded sir.
اچها نانبايى كا واسطے تلاش كر	Seek for a good baker.
اتنا گودا روتي ميں بناوتا كو منع كر	Desire him to make the bread less crummy.
اٹها	Take away.
پالكي كا واسطے حكم دی ميں باهر جاتا	Order the palanqeen, I am going out.
اي بهراو پالكي اورسواري كو تيار كرو صاحب آتا هي	Bearers, get the palanqeen ready and assemble the retinue (our) master is comming.
ــــ صاحب كا گهر كو جاؤ صاحب گهر ميں هي پوچهه	Go to Mr —'s house; inquire if he is at home.

نہیں صاحب باھر گیا	No sir, he is gone out.
کدھر گیا پوچھہ کر	Ask whither he is gone.
وی لگ جانتے نہیں لیکن دو پہر کو پھیر آویگا	They do not know, but he will return at noon.
کتنا باقي هوا	How much does it want?
ڈیڑہ گھڑي	One g,hurry and a half.

DIALOGUE VI.

جنگي کا جواب سوال	*Military.*
صوبه دار لگ صف برابر کراو	Subedars, make even the ranks.
خبر دار سب لگ چوپ رهیں	Take care that all remain silent.
سیدھا کھڑا رهو	Stand straight.
دهینا دیکھو	Look to the right.
مت هیلاو	Don't shuffle.
جیڈهاک کو سنو	Listen to the drum.

Mind to shoulder your firelocks together.	ایکتھا بندوق کاندھا پر رکھنا کو خبردار
Be careful to perform the exercise actively together by the drum.	ایکتھا قواعد کرنا کو جیڈھاک سے چوت پتي خبردار
Let the near ranks close to the front, that the whole battalion fire a volley together.	پیچ لیین صفین خبردار آگت آنا کو ایکتھا چھوڑنا کو سب پلٹن
Observe to wheel from the centre; the men near the centre to move with short steps, those a distance, to march with longer steps.	ناف سے گھومنا کو خبردار آدمیان جو ناف کا نزدیک هیں چھوٹا قدم سی چلنا کو جو تفاوت هیں اور لمبا بناونا کو
All look to the centre and march regularly; mind you don't get before one another.	سب ناف کو دیکھو اور برابر چلو اگی پیچھي مت جاؤ خبردار
Subehdars, attend to the giving of the word of command for exact firings.	صوبه دار لگ خبردار ٹھیک چھوڑنا کو حکم کہي دینا کو

کوچ کرنا کو خبردار دهینا کا پایوں سے شروع کر برابر اور چل زور سے	In marching remember to begin with the right leg, march uniformly with a firm step.
جد تھکانا میں ہوگی تمہاري بندوق سب خوب ساف کراو چکنا کر اچھا طرح صیقل کراو	When you are in quarters, clean your muskets and well polish them.

TERMS OF GRAMMAR.

एक बचन्	ایک بچن	Singular.
भूबचन्	بهو بچن	Plural.
कारक्	کارک	Case.
लिङग	لنگ	Gender.
पुंल्लिङग	پلنگ	Masculine.
स्त्रीलिङग	ستریلنگ	Feminine.
नपुंसक	نپنسک	Neuter.

अभी ابهي Present tense.

गैया گيا Preterite.

آينده ٭ هويگا or زمانه٬ استقبال Future.

اسم Noun.

فعل Verb.

NUMERALS.

١ ٢ ٣ ٤ ٥ ٦ ٧ ٨ ٩ ٠   1 2 3 4 5 6 7 8 9 0

ايك one دو two تين three چار four پانچ five چهه six سات seven آٹهه eight نو nine دس ten اگاره eleven باره twelve تيره thirteen چوده fourteen پندره fifteen سوله sixteen ستره seventeen اٹهاره eighteen انيس nineteen بيس twenty اكيس twenty one بائيس twenty two تيئيس twenty three چوبيس twenty four پنچيس twenty five چهبيس twenty six ستايس twenty seven اٹهاييس twenty eight انتيس twenty nine تيس thirty اكتيس thirty one &c. چاليس forty. پنچاس fifty. ساٹهه sixty. ستر seventy. اسي eighty. نووي ninety. سو one hundred. هزار a thousand.

WEEK-DAYS.

اتور Sunday.

سوم وار or پیر Monday.

منگل Tuesday.

بده Wednesday.

جمعه رات Thursday.

جمعه Friday.

سنیچر Saturday.

MONTHS.

بیساکهه April.

جیتهه May.

اساڑه June.

ساون July

بھادون	August.
آسن	September.
کاتک	October.
اگھن	November.
پوس	December.
ماگھ	January.
پھاگن	February.
چیت	March.

THE END.